CALLED TO
RECONCILIATION

"In an age of despiritualization, greater emphasis is usually placed on social reconciliation than on salvific reconciliation. We tend in these days to ignore the consequences of our having lost the strength of our spiritual connection as we long to repair our relationships with our neighbors of different hues. *Called to Reconciliation* forces us to bring a more holistic vision to our quest to become the beloved community to which God is calling us 'with the fierce urgency of now.'"

—**James A. Forbes**, senior minister emeritus, The Riverside Church, NYC

"In a time of political polarization, Augustine reminds Christians that we are called to reconciliation. That calling is not just an invitation to some; it is a mandate for all (see 2 Cor. 5). Augustine's training as a lawyer and pastor come together as he challenges all of us to find fresh ways to reweave the social fabric. A wonderful accomplishment!"

—**L. Gregory Jones**, president, Belmont University;
author of *Embodying Forgiveness*

"A book for our times. In this well-documented, insightful study, Augustine explores the nature of Christian reconciliation in its biblical, theological, social, and contemporary implications. The book surveys the broad concept of reconciliation while providing important implications for recovering it in church and society here and now."

—**Bill J. Leonard**, professor of divinity emeritus, Wake Forest University

"Augustine has clearly and creatively fixed the issue of countering racism within the context of Scripture, thus claiming the issue as a matter of formation for those who follow Jesus. And too, he turns the reader's attention to the future by articulating a vision of hope that is reconciliation. A wonderful resource for those who seek discernment on the topic of racism via the way of faith in Jesus Christ."

—**Russell Kendrick**, bishop, Episcopal Diocese of the Central Gulf Coast

"Augustine has done the best and most comprehensive job I have yet seen not only of describing the racial divide and challenges in this country but also of giving us a hopeful way forward. Of the eight books I've read in the past eighteen months on the topic of racial justice, this one by far resonates the most with me as something that can bring us together, even in a time of such deep division, around this central biblical and cultural necessity. I couldn't put it down, and it renewed my hope that we not only must, but we can, do this."

—**Timothy M. Smith**, bishop, NC Synod, Evangelical Lutheran Church in America

"In the tradition of theologians such as Walter Rauschenbusch, Howard Thurman, and James Cone, *Called to Reconciliation* is a masterful argument demonstrating that faith is thought and deed. Through the focus on reconciliation, the text provides a clear, biblically based pathway for people to begin to reimagine their connection to others and what this requires of them. This book could easily be applied to classrooms, church groups, and social organizations. In the midst of the intense and never-ending culture war that has erupted in response to the successes of the civil rights movement, this text provides an explanation of why this has happened and a vision of how to end the enduring and painful American internal conflict."

—**Eric L. McDaniel**, associate professor, University of Texas at Austin; author of *Politics in the Pews*

"An important book and a timely book. Augustine draws the call to reconciliation from the very heart of the gospel of Jesus Christ. What has been far too peripheral (where it has even existed) in the American evangelical church has been summoned to the center of the church's life. I commend this work to pastors, to church study groups, and to the college and seminary classroom."

—**R. Robert Creech**, professor and director of pastoral ministries, George W. Truett Theological Seminary, Baylor University

"Augustine has issued a call to the church to engage its diversity, or sad lack of it, if it is to take up the all-important work of reconciliation. Augustine's mastery of theology, political theory, sociology, and the law enables him to describe a path forward. It is way past time for our congregations to give up on their segregated ways and become beacons and witnesses for true reconciliation. For any in the church looking for a partner in the Christian vocation of reconciliation, they will find one in this author and be enriched by his wisdom and passion."

—**David M. Greenhaw**, president emeritus, Eden Theological Seminary

"Augustine's multidisciplinary work is a gift to the church, by which I mean the diverse *ekklēsia* envisioned by Jesus. Drawing on and synthesizing a wide array of resources from theology, politics, and law, Augustine has written a powerful and inspiring book for individual Christians and congregations ready to work for reconciliation. He calls the church to lead in our society's larger fight to end systemic racism by recovering the heart of a Gospel message that affirms the equal worth and dignity of all people."

—**Amanda Tyler**, executive director, Baptist Joint Committee for Religious Liberty

"This masterful work is an essential tool for all people of good will as we seek solutions to the serious and deep fissures challenging our society. A road map for how we come together when we seem so far apart, this is a must-read for anyone navigating the intersection of faith and politics."

—**Leah D. Daughtry**, national presiding prelate of The House of the Lord Churches, author, and activist-organizer

CALLED TO
RECONCILIATION

HOW THE CHURCH CAN MODEL
JUSTICE, DIVERSITY, AND INCLUSION

JONATHAN C. AUGUSTINE

Foreword by WILLIAM H. WILLIMON
Afterword by MICHAEL B. CURRY

Baker Academic
a division of Baker Publishing Group
Grand Rapids, Michigan

© 2022 by Jonathan C. Augustine

Published by Baker Academic
a division of Baker Publishing Group
PO Box 6287, Grand Rapids, MI 49516-6287
www.bakeracademic.com

Printed in the United States of America

Library of Congress Cataloging-in-Publication Data
Names: Augustine, Jonathan C., 1971– author.
Title: Called to reconciliation : how the church can model justice, diversity, and inclusion / Jonathan C. Augustine ; foreword by William H. Willimon ; afterword by Michael B. Curry.
Description: Grand Rapids, Michigan : Baker Academic, a division of Baker Publishing Group, [2022] | Includes index.
Identifiers: LCCN 2021040518 | ISBN 9781540965035 (paperback) | ISBN 9781540965257 (casebound) | ISBN 9781493435371 (ebook) | ISBN 9781493435388 (pdf)
Subjects: LCSH: Reconciliation—Religious aspects—Christianity.
Classification: LCC BT738.27 .A94 2022 | DDC 234/.5—dc23
LC record available at https://lccn.loc.gov/2021040518

Baker Publishing Group publications use paper produced from sustainable forestry practices and post-consumer waste whenever possible.

22   23   24   25   26   27   28   7   6   5   4   3   2   1

To the memory of my precious mother,
Jeanne Cunningham Augustine (1930–2020)

CONTENTS

FOREWORD

Here's the right book, at the right time, written by the right person, for the right reasons. Lots of folks are talking about and yearning for racial reconciliation. Jay Augustine joins that conversation and debate by boldly speaking up for reconciliation from an unashamed, uniquely Christian point of view.

Jay adheres to a "gumbo" view of diversity. (For all of us not from Louisiana, Jay explains, "Good gumbo is good because it's made with a variety of diverse ingredients, each one enriching the others.") He believes that "society is also better when it brings diverse people and diverse groups together." Then Jay moves into a Christian, richly biblical defense of diversity, and, before he is done, he also offers guidance for how to achieve diversity in our churches for the sake of the world.

While informed by current sociological, systemic, and critical theory accounts of our racialized culture, Jay dives right into theology, confident that our christological convictions have real-life, here-and-now consequences. The whole New Testament is a response to the early church's shock and awe that God's salvation had exploded out from God's people, Israel, to include even us gentiles. In your church and mine, God is busy gathering a people that looks different from the divisions, separations, and bogus, dehumanizing ploys of the world. Every Christian, in every age, recapitulates Peter's encounter with Cornelius in Acts 10. We who have been and are being reconciled to

God in Christ are thereby free to expect and delight in our reconciliation to one another.

Though he is thoroughly aware of the problematic aspects of the
calls of white Christians for "reconciliation" with Black Christians
(when, in America's history of white and Black, were we ever concili-
ated? he asks), knowing that pleas for reconciliation can be various
forms of manipulation by the powerful, Jay still argues that reconciliation is at the heart of the Christian hope and witness.

Christ puts pressure on his people to expect and work for diversity
and to show the world what diversity looks like. Jesus Christ is not
only reconciler but also the one who convenes a people (the church)
whose members become active agents of reconciliation. Examining
the Gospels' depiction of Jesus as boundary-breaking reconciler, then
deep-diving into Paul's challenge for early congregations to become
showcases for God's reconciliation (especially in 1 Cor. 11:17–22
and Gal. 3:26–28), Jay shows that "issues of justice, diversity, and
reconciliation are not extra add-ons that the church can opt out of
as a matter of personal preference. They are an essential part of the
gospel."[1] Indeed, as an announcement of who God is and what God
is up to in the world, the gospel, in both content and effect, is about
reconciliation.

Paul stressed the "kingdom at hand" as strongly as he stressed
the "kingdom to come." Christ gathers us in order that the church
might be a showcase for what Christ is able to work in the world
here, now, despite all the ways we try to separate from and divide one
another. Through an astute reading of Paul's Letter to the Romans,
Jay detects a "vertical" plane, representing humanity's reconciled
relationship with God (salvific reconciliation), and a "horizontal"
plane, representing human beings' reconciled relationships with one
another (social reconciliation). Christ is about reconciliation on both
planes, promising a gumbo sort of church if we are faithful to his
invitation to work with him. Salvific and social reconciliation then
work together to enact civil reconciliation, which is primarily secular
in intent and scope but is rooted in Paul's theology of equality.

1. John M. Perkins, *One Blood: Parting Words to the Church on Race and Love*
(Chicago: Moody, 2018), 19–20.

Jay enables the ancient witness of the church to be as relevant and contemporary as the Black Lives Matter movement. He sets forth a challenge for how we do church as well as for how we conduct our politics.

I'm sure that you will find *Called to Reconciliation* to be just what you need to equip yourself for living into the shock that, in Christ, God is reconciling the whole world to God and reconciling us all to one another (2 Cor. 5:19).

William H. Willimon
Retired Bishop, United Methodist Church
Professor of the Practice of Christian Ministry, Duke Divinity School

ACKNOWLEDGMENTS

There are several institutions and individuals to whom I owe thanks. Although *Called to Reconciliation* is the product of my individual labor, it was made possible by support systems that encouraged and nurtured me in ways beyond expression.

I entered Duke University's Doctor of Ministry program in August 2017. As someone deeply grounded in the Christian faith, I was especially grateful for intimate worship at the beautiful Duke chapel. I was indeed drawn in by the chapel's architectural design and ornate stone carvings. One carving, at the chapel's entrance, was of Robert E. Lee, the general who commanded the Confederate Army during the American Civil War.

In what seemed like only hours after I left the chapel service that began my doctoral program, an undercurrent of divisiveness—largely centered on race—once again enveloped the United States. It was only three months earlier, in May 2017, while serving as the general (international) chaplain of Alpha Phi Alpha Fraternity Inc. and senior pastor of Historic St. James AME Church in downtown New Orleans, that I led the fraternity in an organized prayer vigil to pray for the removal of Confederate monuments from public view. Our nonviolent, prayerful efforts were successful in that, in a matter of days, the city's mayor removed monuments of Jefferson Davis, P. G. T. Beauregard, and Robert E. Lee. By August 2017, however, the country's temperament was *not* prayerful. It was violent. Indeed, a violent and deadly public protest broke out in Charlottesville, Virginia.

After tensions flared between white-supremacist neo-Nazis and antiracist activists, the forty-fifth president of the United States—often accused of being racist because of outlandish comments—stoked the flames by attributing fault to "both sides." During this unfolding drama, I really began to understand the depths of inclusivity at Duke. President Vincent Price, who had become the university's tenth president only one month before, took the bold leadership step of having the statute of Lee removed from campus. Price's leadership was both bold and reassuring. It reassured me, as an African American male, that I was welcome at an institution that would shape my thinking and public proclamation. Equally reassuring was Bishop Will Willimon, my professor and program director. For his faithful witness to the ministry of reconciliation and the cause of social justice, I will forever be thankful.

I was blessed to serve two congregations that supported my matriculation at Duke: Historic St. James AME Church, in New Orleans, and St. Joseph AME Church, in Durham. My service through them allowed me to grow as a minister and befriend some wonderful people. I am immeasurably thankful for their support. Further, I am thankful to the two bishops who appointed me to serve those historic congregations: Bishop Julius Harrison McAllister Sr. appointed me to Historic St. James in November 2015, and Bishop James Levert Davis appointed me to St. Joseph in May 2019.

I am also deeply thankful to Greg Jones, the president of Belmont University, who supervised my work during his service as dean of Duke Divinity School. I benefited tremendously from Greg's thought-provoking writings, insightful edits, constructive criticisms, and consistent encouragement. Our efforts produced a work that will serve both the church and the academy. I am also thankful to Kimberly Hewitt, Duke's vice president for institutional equity and chief diversity officer. *Called to Reconciliation* moves from an academic focus, defining the church's theology of reconciliation, to explore reconciliation practically, through efforts aimed at diversity and inclusion. I benefited from Kim's insight as a talented lawyer and higher-education diversity professional.

Equally as important, I am also thankful for conversations with and editorial suggestions from my lifelong friend Rory Verrett. Rory's insights helped shape my conceptualization of how to bring together theories of diversity and inclusion that range from the apostolic era to the modern day, a span of more than two thousand years. I benefited from both the informality of our conversations and the structural and stylistic edits Rory suggested. Ultimately, I am grateful the editors at Baker Academic selected my work for publication. Specifically, I will always be thankful for having worked with a team of such quality professionals, particularly Dave Nelson and Alex DeMarco.

Finally, I am thankful to my family, especially my wife and children, as well as my sister, for her comments on earlier drafts of my manuscript. Regretfully, before this book was published, my dear mother transitioned to eternity. I am thankful for the blessing of being her son, and it is to her precious memory that this book is respectfully dedicated.

INTRODUCTION

Now faith is the assurance of things hoped for, the conviction of things not seen. —Hebrews 11:1

I grew up in New Orleans, and I love gumbo. Better stated: I love *good* gumbo. What makes a gumbo *good*? Some might say the seafood. Others might say the seasonings. Still others might even say the roux. As one of New Orleans's most popular foods, gumbo typically contains seafood *and* seasonings, and all gumbo begins with a roux. *Good* gumbo, however, incorporates difference.

Good gumbo is good because it's made with a variety of diverse ingredients, each one enriching the others. I believe society is also better when it brings diverse people and diverse groups together in community because our perspectives and experiences are enriched by differences. If diversity is good for society, then it must also be good for the church! In the following pages, while I emphasize the importance of diversity and inclusion, with an egalitarian respect for all people and traditions, I also connect theology, legal history, and politics with diversity and inclusion practices. I link them through a discussion of reconciliation at a time when the United States of America is anything but reconciled.

During the Civil Rights Movement of the 1950s and '60s, Reverend Dr. Martin Luther King Jr. led the Black church in moving toward reconciliation. King sought reconciliation between Blacks and whites amid widespread enmity, as Jim Crow laws subjugated Blacks to a caste system that marginalized Black existence. Although laws may have changed, the systemic social barriers that marginalize minorities have persisted, as evidenced by the circumstances giving rise to the many Black Lives Matter protests throughout the United States beginning in 2013.

The names Breonna Taylor, Ahmaud Arbery, and George Floyd will forever do more than remind Americans of generational racial disparities. Their names are exhibit A in making the case that America must move toward reconciliation, racial and otherwise. As evidence that hope can always be found during despair, very clear demographic differences between the protesters of the 1960s and the protesters of the last few years suggest the United States now has an opportunity to move toward reconciliation by bringing diverse groups together. The modern-day Black Lives Matter protests are not majority Black—a visible opposition to the American caste system that has castigated and marginalized Blacks. Protesters are now people of all colors and races. Indeed, the rebirthed Black Lives Matter movement of 2020 proves that if *all lives* really do matter, *Black lives* must matter too.

Problems associated with racial discrimination cannot be unilaterally solved by Blacks, no more so than problems associated with gender discrimination can be independently solved by women. True reconciliation cannot be done alone. It requires diverse people coming together, just like diverse ingredients come together in gumbo. The Black Lives Matter movement brought together people of all races, as well as corporate giants and nonprofit community organizers, in the seeking of social equity. More importantly, however, 2020's moment of reckoning—after a white Minneapolis police officer killed George Floyd by keeping his knee on Floyd's neck for nine minutes and twenty-nine seconds—clearly showed that America's social problems are better addressed when disparate groups come together to work in community. By doing so, groups have left identity politics behind to engage in equity practices aimed at reconciliation.

As a counterargument, some claim that the concept of racial reconciliation is a misnomer, because America's history of pervasive racism shows that there has never truly been "conciliation"—a relationship of unity and harmony between whites and persons of color—in this country.[1] Indeed, assuming that racial reconciliation is an attempt to restore a mythical harmony, which never existed, distorts and conceals the truth about America's sordid past. What some "woke" non-Blacks have recently been made to realize—through books like Robin DiAngelo's *White Fragility*[2] and tragedies like the violent killings of Taylor, Arbery, and Floyd—is that telling the truth means owning America's post-Reconstruction history of disenfranchising, marginalizing, and imprisoning Blacks, including the Jim Crow system of racial segregation made possible by the Supreme Court's infamous ruling in *Plessy v. Ferguson* (1896) establishing the "separate but [un]equal" doctrine, which had devastating social, educational, and economic repercussions. Owning America's truth is a requisite for moving toward reconciliation.

In a similar vein, after the evil institution of apartheid came to an end in South Africa and Nelson Mandela became the country's first democratically elected president, in 1994, Archbishop Desmond Tutu was appointed to lead the South African Truth and Reconciliation Commission, a task force whose job it was to face the truth of South Africa's past in order to forge a common path forward for the future. In *No Future without Forgiveness*, Tutu describes how the commission's work toward reconciliation was not at all concerned with *retributive justice*, where the goal is punitive.[3] Instead, the commission's chief goal was *restorative justice*, where instead of retribution or punishment, "the central concern is the healing of breaches, the redressing of imbalances, the restoration of broken relationships, a seeking to rehabilitate both the victim and the perpetrator, who should be given the opportunity to be reintegrated into the community he has injured by his offense."[4] If the United States is also to move toward reconciliation, its social problems must likewise be addressed with honesty, by diverse groups coming together to create something new. Gumbo anyone?

1. Douglas A. Foster, "Reclaiming Reconciliation: The Corruption of 'Racial Reconciliation' and How It Might Be Reclaimed for Racial Justice and Unity," *Journal of Ecumenical Studies* 55, no. 1 (2020): 63–81.

2. Robin DiAngelo, *White Fragility: Why It's So Hard for White People to Talk about Racism* (Boston: Beacon, 2018).

3. Desmond Tutu, *No Future without Forgiveness* (New York: Doubleday Books, 1999), 54.

4. Tutu, *No Future without Forgiveness*, 54–55.

Reconciliation in Context

Reconciliation is one of the rare words that originates within the church but that also applies in secular contexts. From a perspective with Christ at the center, it has to do with humans being reconciled to God *through Jesus*. This is what I call *salvific reconciliation* because it relates to human salvation. In the closely related social context, reconciliation also has to do with humans being reconciled to one another, as equals, *because of Jesus's saving work*. I call this *social reconciliation*. What's the difference between the two? Whereas salvific reconciliation is focused on the "kingdom to come" (i.e., it is soteriological or eschatological), social reconciliation is part of the here and now and is focused on the "kingdom at hand" (e.g., on systemic social inequities). My focus herein is not so much on salvation or the concept of heaven. I focus instead on an egalitarian ethic—that is, on social equality: different groups embracing "the Other" in a mutually beneficial and diverse community. Stated otherwise, social reconciliation looks like good gumbo.

Before going further, to appropriately place my use of the term *reconciliation* in context, as it relates to the construct of race in America, I find it helpful to distinguish between reconciliation and equity. Efforts at racial equity seek to remedy the structural racism historically embedded in America's cultural, political, social, and economic systems and institutions by seeking just and fair inclusion that allows all people to participate in society and reach their full potential.[5] Reconciliation seeks to restore broken relationship by finding commonality as humans who are all created in God's image. While equity is primarily secular, reconciliation begins in a religious ethos and progresses to include secular communities.

In the pages that follow, I set forth a theological basis for reconciliation by identifying a scriptural trajectory linking the leadership of Peter (Matt. 16:13–19; Acts 2; 10) with the theology of Paul, illustrating how disparate groups can create community. This link makes for a gumbo-like variety that is rooted in equitable human relations (see

---

5. See Angela Glover Blackwell et al., *The Competitive Advantage of Racial Equity*, https://www.policylink.org/sites/default/files/The%20Competitive%20Advantage%20of%20Racial%20Equity-final_0.pdf.

1 Cor. 11:17–22). Moreover, this theology of equality is not only a core component of social reconciliation in Paul's letters but also the basis for an ethical derivative of them, what I call *civil reconciliation.* Civil reconciliation is what presumably fueled the Reverend Oliver Brown in *Brown v. Board of Education* (1954) and the then-barely-known Reverend Martin Luther King Jr. in prophetically leading the Black church into the politics of the Civil Rights Movement. Insofar as social reconciliation embraces a fellowship that is no respecter of persons (Acts 10:34), civil reconciliation demands governmental and legal redress by placing different groups of people in community with one another. Stated otherwise, gumbo is not supposed to be a homogeneous soup but a richly diverse delicacy.

Consider Rev. Brown. As a minister at St. Mark's African Methodist Episcopal Church in Topeka, Kansas, Brown served in a denomination founded because of legal racial inequities and a desire for human equality.[6] Brown sued the Topeka Board of Education on behalf of his daughter, Linda, who was denied admission to a local school because she was Black. Describing the circumstances leading to litigation, legal scholars write, "The lead plaintiff, Oliver Brown, was . . . angered that his daughter had to travel each day past a modern, fully equipped white school to a black school housed in a deteriorated building."[7] By therefore filing suit, Rev. Brown, although he believed in salvation in the "kingdom to come," sought to address systemic social inequities rooted in America's legal system in the "kingdom at hand."

The *Brown* case was consolidated with four others to be brought before the US Supreme Court. On May 17, 1954, the Court sided with Rev. Brown and the plaintiffs, declaring that segregation in public

6. The African Methodist Episcopal Church, the oldest predominately Black denomination, originates from a 1787 breakaway from what was then the Methodist Episcopal Church (the precursor to the United Methodist Church) in Philadelphia. African American worshipers formed the Free African Society, a precursor to the legal establishment of the AMEC, because they were discriminated against during worship. See Richard S. Newman, *Freedom's Prophet: Bishop Richard Allen, the AME Church, and the Black Founding Fathers* (New York: New York University Press, 2008), 173–76.

7. Robert J. Cottrol, Raymond T. Diamond, and Leland B. Ware, *Brown v. Board of Education: Caste, Culture, and the Constitution* (Lawrence: University Press of Kansas, 2003), 128.

education is unconstitutional. Accordingly, one of history's most famous Supreme Court cases came about because a minister fought for civil reconciliation, demanding equitable treatment for his daughter.

In regard to the social aspect of reconciliation, as exhibited in Paul's letters, and the secular aspect of civil reconciliation, as exhibited by Rev. Oliver Brown, I believe no greater example exists of how the former influenced the latter than the Civil Rights Movement's fight for equality and acceptance, which put into practice Paul's theology of equality. America's segregated schools were a daily reminder that society had not yet embraced reconciliation. In theory, at least, the Supreme Court's ruling in *Brown* would lead to gumbo-like diversity in America by opening school doors to Blacks. In actuality, the pushback over *Brown* served as an impetus for the Civil Rights Movement, setting the stage for America to meet another minister—this time in Montgomery, Alabama, about eighteen months later—who also demonstrated a belief in human equality.

Rev. Martin Luther King Jr. (then just twenty-six years old) preached a liberationist gospel that focused not only on the fact that *Jesus died* but also on the fact that *Jesus lived*. King reminded the oppressed and their oppressors that Jesus's ministry was anchored in social liberation. Indeed, as Jesus's ministry began, he publicly professed, "The Spirit of the Lord is upon me, because he has anointed me to bring good news to the poor. He has sent me to proclaim release to the captives and recovery of sight to the blind, to let the oppressed go free, to proclaim the year of the Lord's favor" (Luke 4:18–19). Inspired by this example of liberationist ministry, King also sought to liberate the oppressed by challenging unjust laws with the Montgomery Bus Boycott.

King's work toward civil reconciliation produced two easily observable and successful measures: (1) passage of the Voting Rights Act of 1965 and (2) adoption of the government's policy on affirmative action. Both measures sought to foster reconciliation by bringing diverse people together for communal benefit. Peter had done the same thing when he baptized Cornelius, the first gentile member of the church (Acts 10:44–48).

So, back to the stove. *Good* gumbo might contain shrimp *and* crab meat along with chicken *and* sausage. It's not simply enough to have seafood and meat. Different *types of seafood* and different *types of meat* make for good gumbo, just as different *types of people* and *different types of perspectives from different types of people* make for a cohesively functioning society and church.

The Divided States of America

Notwithstanding the Civil Rights Movement's success with civil reconciliation, some factions within the United States openly want a country that's as bland as broth—nothing like a good gumbo.[8] This reality became especially evident through the "Make America Great Again" political narrative that drove Donald Trump's 2016 election to the presidency and continued to foster divisions in the church, especially between conservative white evangelicals and progressive Black Protestants. As the political pendulum swung from Barack Obama to Donald Trump, white nationalist and neo-Nazi forces, which had been brewing during Obama's presidency, contributed significantly to Trump's election.[9] Those factions were also emboldened to lead antiminority spectacles, like the one in August 2017 in Charlottesville, Virginia.[10] Further, the incendiary Make America Great Again political narrative also led to a rise in hate crimes.[11] This empirically

8. As an example, on the morning of October 27, 2018, only days before the 2018 midterm elections, an anti-Semitic white nationalist entered the Tree of Life Synagogue in Pittsburgh and killed eleven Jewish worshipers. See Matt Zapotosky, Devlin Barnett, and Mark Berman, "Suspect in Pittsburg Synagogue Shooting Is Charged in 44-Count Hate-Crime Indictment," *Washington Post*, October 31, 2018, https:// www.washingtonpost.com/world/national-security/suspect-in-pittsburgh-synagogue -shooting-charged-in-44-count-hate-crime-indictment/2018/10/31/bf2be61c-dd36 -11e8-b3f0-62607289efee_story.html?utm_term=.0ea4949b543c.

9. Amanda Graham et al., "Who Wears the MAGA Hat? Racial Beliefs and Faith in Trump," *Socius* 7 (March 2021): 1–16.

10. Michael D. Shear and Maggie Haberman, "Trump Again Defends Initial Remarks on Charlottesville; Again, Blames 'Both Sides,'" *New York Times*, August 15, 2017, https://www.nytimes.com/2017/08/15/us/politics/trump-press-conference -charlottesville.html.

11. See, e.g., Meg Oliver, "Pittsburg Shooting Highlights Rise in Hate Crimes across the U.S.," CBS Evening News, October 28, 2018, https://www.cbsnews.com /news/pittsburgh-shooting-highlights-rise-hate-crimes-united-states; and Yascha Mounk, "The Nature of Trump's Culpability in the Pittsburgh Synagogue Massacre: The Shooter May Despise Him, but the President's Dehumanizing Language Has

measured increase underscores the dramatic divisions and factions within the United States that have become even more pronounced in recent years. Several of those divisions emanate from the church.

Some of America's church-based divisions are denominational. Accordingly, differences in orthodoxy are expected. Other divisions are historically social, like those between Blacks and whites. Remember, for example, King's still sad maxim that "11 a.m. on Sunday mornings is the most segregated hour in America." I focus, however, on some theological divisions, such as those between conservative evangelicals and more liberal, mainline Christians. Such divisions, like those over a woman's right to choose, under *Roe v. Wade* (1973), have been at the heart of public policy debates, worsening religious and social divisions in the United States for more than forty years.

The counternarrative to more conservative and dogmatic theologies has come from progressive and emancipatory faith traditions, including those within the Black church that rose to prominence during the Civil Rights Movement. The Black church led the way in basing civil reconciliation in an ethic of equality, premised on the social reconciliation in Paul's letters. Civil reconciliation places great value on diversity in American life while seeking to enforce the ethic of equality through governmental intervention and prophetic resistance. It is this same resistance that is at the heart of the Black Lives Matter movement.

Social Divisions and the Church's Ministry of Reconciliation

In a time marked by so much xenophobia and racial, religious, and social division, the church's ministry of reconciliation is especially

Made Political Violence—and Hate Crimes Like This—More Likely," *Slate*, October 27, 2018, https://slate.com/news-and-politics/2018/10/pittsburgh-synagogue-shooting-trump-rhetoric-antisemitism-civility.html. See also Media Advisory Press Release, "NAACP Sees Rise in Hate Crimes, Legacy of Trump's Racism," June 29, 2018, https://www.naacp.org/latest/naacp-sees-continued-rise-hate-crimes-legacy-trumps-racism; and Joshua Holland, "Yes, Donald Trump Is Making White People More Hateful: A New Study Finds Empirical Evidence of the 'Trump Effect,'" *The Nation*, May 2, 2018, https://www.thenation.com/article/yes-donald-trump-is-making-white-people-more-hateful.

urgent. The church today must repent of her divisions and return to her apostolic-era theology of equality to realize God's intention, as evidenced in Scripture, for a diverse and inclusive community of belonging. Doing so will allow the church to be an exemplar for society. Further, just as society can benefit from the church returning to a theology of equality, so the church can benefit from secular-world diversity and inclusion practices that value heterogeneity.

In what follows, I conduct a multidisciplinary analysis that is rooted in theology, legal history, and diversity and inclusion principles. I begin with theological foundations and move through both historical and present-day analyses before connecting the church's apostolic-era theology of equality with diversity principles within today's society and practices of inclusion.

Part 1: The Theology of Reconciliation

Part 1 establishes a foundation for society to learn from the church's evolving paradigm of reconciliation with "the Other." This part defines and connects salvific and social reconciliation, both foundationally anchored in six biblical texts—Matthew 16:13–19; Acts 2; 10; Romans 5–8; 1 Corinthians 11:17–22; Galatians 3:26–28—before examining a biblical trajectory that is rooted in the church's origins and evolution. Part 1 explores Peter's leadership and Paul's theology alongside the Civil Rights Movement's use of King as an exemplar in leading the Black church toward civil reconciliation.

Chapter 1 establishes a foundation for social reconciliation by looking at the word *church* (*ekklēsia*) as originally introduced in Matthew 16:13–19, when Jesus calls Peter the rock upon which Jesus will build the church. Although social reconciliation is at the core of Paul's theology, it begins with Peter's leadership and goes through a chronological progression in Scripture. In Matthew 16:13–19 (this extract, or pericope, is labeled "Peter's Declaration about Jesus" or "Peter's Confession"), Jesus responds to Peter's indication of Jesus's lordship by rewarding Peter's faithfulness: "Flesh and blood has not revealed this to you, but my Father in heaven. . . . You are Peter, and on this rock I will build my church" (16:17–18). This is the first time the word *church* (*ekklēsia*) appears in Scripture. Literally meaning an "assembly" or "group," Jesus's reference is not to a physical structure with a steeple and vestibule but to an assembly of people, or the "body of Christ." Jesus intended this group, this *ekklēsia*, to be diverse.

With Peter designated to lead from a special place of honor in building the church, the book of Acts provides an early church history. Luke, its presumed author, tells of Peter's preaching on the day of Pentecost, when thousands joined the church (Acts 2). Indeed, those who joined and accepted Christ as the foretold Messiah did not join a building. They joined the *ekklēsia*. Although the Pentecost narrative describes the diversity of those who joined the assembly, its original members were all Jews (2:5). The original church, therefore, began as a religiously homogeneous entity—unlike a richly diverse gumbo and more like a bland broth—that had not yet engaged in reconciliation with "the Other." Under Peter's leadership, however, the church's ethnic composition changed.

In Acts 10, before the New Testament progresses to the church's ministry of reconciliation in Paul's letters, a biblical version of unconscious bias appears. This is the same cognitive phenomenon that continually plagues society. When people make and manipulate stereotypes based on ethnicity, gender, religion, or sexual orientation and unknowingly treat people unlike them as "the Other," they are drawing on and perpetuating unconscious bias. Indeed, they have the same reaction to social equity work that the Jewish Peter had after dreaming of the divisions between Jews and gentiles being overcome (Acts 10:9–16): "By no means, Lord." It was not until Peter rejected his bias and embraced the gentile Cornelius as his equal that the church started moving toward reconciliation. This egalitarian ethic became the ethos of Paul's theology. Accordingly, before exploring the social dimensions of Paul's theology in chapter 2, I lay a foundation in chapter 1 that details Peter's leadership in facilitating reconciliation between Jews and gentiles based on a divine revelation that Jesus came for *all* people.

Chapter 2 builds on the foundational exploration of Peter's leadership in chapter 1 by looking at Paul's theology. By exploring Paul's "theology of equality," most popularly manifested in Galatians 3:26–28, 1 Corinthians 11:17–22, and Romans 5–8, I provide a historical contextualization of social reconciliation. I argue that this type of reconciliation with the proverbial "Other," rooted in a Pauline theology of equitable relations within the church, lies at the heart of Paul's authentic writings.

Chapter 3 moves from biblical examples of social reconciliation to placing Paul's theology of equality in the context of *civil reconciliation*. Martin Luther King Jr.'s leadership in the Civil Rights Movement was an example of Paul's theology in practical application, as are the protests of today's Black Lives Matter activists. As these examples show, civil reconciliation essentially applies Paul's theology of equality in the form of demands for governmental redress. This remedy ensures that equitable treatment is not only moral but also legal.

Chapter 3 also focuses on forgiveness. True reconciliation requires that dominant and subjugated groups (such as whites and Blacks) wipe the slate clean, as Bishop Tutu exhorted the citizens of South Africa to do after the hard work of the Truth and Reconciliation Commission. Thus the church's work toward civil reconciliation must continue. Indeed, this is the ministry that Jesus left to the church (2 Cor. 5:17–19). As a body moving toward reconciliation, the church should continue its witness of transformation by working for more just and equitable political and socioeconomic systems in society.

Part 2: Reconciliation with "the Other"

Chapter 4 covers the reaction to progress made by the Black church with passage of the Voting Rights Act of 1965 and the government's adoption of affirmative action, two of the Civil Rights Movement's most quantifiable measures of success, at least in terms of diversity and inclusion. In the late 1960s, Richard Nixon's presidential campaign engaged in a "southern strategy," which sought to align conservative voters with white evangelical Christians in rejecting the racial progress associated with civil reconciliation. This conservative alliance, known as the Religious Right, proved to be a bedrock Republican Party constituency, especially after Ronald Reagan famously courted evangelicals in his successful 1980 presidential campaign.

Chapter 4 highlights that this same conservative alliance, almost unified in opposition to abortion, as allowed under *Roe v. Wade* (1973), led to Trump's 2016 election, as conservative white evangelicals embraced the Make America Great Again narrative, the very antithesis of anything associated with reconciliation. Now, however, the extremity of Trump's politics and policies has created a public break among evangelicals that has not existed for at least forty years. In moving the church toward reconciliation, we must ask whether this division in evangelicalism presents an opportunity, albeit qualified, for more progressive evangelicals to find common ground with mainline Christians, including the Black church, on issues such as the environment, food insecurity, and racial reconciliation.

Chapter 5 concludes part 2 by asking again the proverbial question Martin Luther King Jr. asked after the Civil Rights Movement had achieved some success: *Where do we go from here?* By exploring diversity in Revelation's "church militant" and "church triumphant," I argue that God intends for the *ekklēsia* to be diverse. God intends for the church to welcome all people. God intends for the church to include all immigrants vilified in the Make America Great Again political narrative. God intends for the church to be a place of racial and ethnic heterogeneity where different people can celebrate diversity. Accordingly, chapter 5 connects the church with traditionally secular practices of diversity and inclusion. This link shows the benefits of diversity for a church seeking to develop a common space, largely driven by social issues, where evangelicals and mainline Christians can move toward reconciliation to improve society. While Trump's divisive political narrative bleats to "Make America Great Again," by calling the church to return to her apostolic-era embrace of "the Other," chapter 5 challenges us to make the church great again.

Because the majority of this book's five chapters were written prior to the November 2020 presidential election, chapter 5 is followed by an epilogue in which I seek to supplement my original research and arguments with a factual analysis of how certain occurrences either collapsed or cemented racial lines of division and what effect those occurrences had on the movement toward reconciliation. Did controversial policies, like separating migrant children from their families at the US/Mexico border and placing them in cages for indeterminate periods of time, create divisions among evangelical voters and move some of them closer to mainline Christians? What impact did the resurged Black Lives Matter movement, in aligning with other nonprofit advocacy organizations and more progressive evangelical voters, have on the election and on the politicization of the Black church? And how did the disparate impact of the COVID-19 pandemic either increase or decrease racial polarization between white evangelicals and the Black church?

Conclusion

The leadership of the Civil Rights Movement showed the world that faith compels social action. The Scripture passage cited in the epigraph states that faith is the evidence of things not seen. The United States of America has not before seen opportunities for large-scale reconciliation like those that manifested in 2020. By arguing that it's time to *make the church great again*, I imply that the United States is too fractured—partially because of divisions emanating from the church—*not* to engage in systemic social reforms. The church must continue the ministry of reconciliation that Jesus left to her. Her contemporary work necessitates prophetic, public engagement to create common ground. With the church faithfully calling out systemic social inequities, America has a real chance of moving toward reconciliation.

PART 1

THE THEOLOGY OF
RECONCILIATION

ONE

THE TRAJECTORY OF RECONCILIATION

Definitions and Peter's Leadership
in the Early Church

Then Peter began to speak to them: "I truly understand that God shows no partiality, but in every nation anyone who fears him and does what is right is acceptable to him." —Acts 10:34–35

Defining and Contextualizing Reconciliation: Salvific, Social, and Civil

The term *reconciliation* entered the English lexicon after its use in Greek throughout the Mediterranean in the first and second centuries. In a secular sense, the term might mean mediation between parties that come together in peace and give up their enmity.[1] In a theological context, however, reconciliation—similar to the concept of atonement—denotes humans being restored in their relationship with God. Since the late twentieth century, peacemaking practices centered on reconciliation have offered ways to curtail the effects of violence and war in society. Indeed, because of the popularity of entities like the South African Truth and Reconciliation Commission,

1. Svetlana Khobnya, "Reconciliation Must Prevail: A Fresh Look at 2 Corinthians 5:14–6:2," *European Journal of Theology* 25, no. 2 (2016): 129.

as well as various denominational "ministries of reconciliation," the term is frequently used in popular culture.

Although reconciliation's theological underpinnings are arguably a core component of the New Testament, the Greek words meaning "to reconcile" and "reconciliation" appear only thirteen times in the Bible, almost exclusively in Paul's letters.[2] Moreover, when we distinguish between the writings that are believed to be authentically Paul's and those believed to be written by other, anonymous authors, we find that variations of the term appear in Paul's authentic letters only in the Corinthian correspondence and in Romans (1 Cor. 7:11; 2 Cor. 5:18–19; Rom. 5:10–11).[3] The only other places where forms of the word *reconciliation* are used in Scripture are in Matthew and Acts.[4]

Further, of the six times the verb *katallassō* ("to reconcile") is used in Paul's letters, five are in reference to the relationship between God

2. The Greek word translated "to reconcile," *katallassō*, is found six times (Rom. 5:10 [twice], 11; 1 Cor. 7:11; 2 Cor. 5:18, 19). The noun *katallagē* ("reconciliation") is found four times (Rom. 5:11; 11:15; 2 Cor. 5:18, 19). And the related verb *apokatallassō* ("reconcile") is used three times in the deutero-Pauline letters (Eph. 2:16; Col. 1:20, 22). John T. Fitzgerald, "Paul and Paradigm Shifts: Reconciliation and Its Linkage Group," in *Paul beyond the Judaism/Hellenism Divide*, ed. Troels Engberg-Pederson (Louisville: Westminster John Knox, 2001), 241–42. See also Corneliu Constantineanu, *The Social Significance of Reconciliation in Paul's Theology: Narrative Readings in Romans* (London: T&T Clark, 2010), 25; and Ralph P. Martin, *Reconciliation: A Study of Paul's Theology* (Grand Rapids: Academie Books, 1989), 72–73, 80.

3. Scholars have long regarded the Pauline corpus as being composed of both authentic and disputed (deutero-Pauline) epistles. Romans, 1 and 2 Corinthians, Galatians, Philippians, 1 Thessalonians, and Philemon are considered authentic (i.e., to have been written by Paul). Conversely, Ephesians, Colossians, 2 Thessalonians, Hebrews, and the letters to Titus and Timothy are part of the Pauline corpus but not considered authentic. See, e.g., Bruce J. Malina and John J. Pilch, *Social Science Commentary on the Letters of Paul* (Minneapolis: Fortress, 2006), 1. Accordingly, with respect to Paul's use of forms of the word *reconciliation*, only the Corinthian correspondence and Romans are considered to be authentic. See Delbert Royce Burkett, *An Introduction to the New Testament and the Origins of Christianity* (Cambridge: Cambridge University Press, 2002), 292–93.

4. The related word *diallassomai* in Matt. 5:24 means "become reconciled," referring to reconciliation with one's brother or sister before an altar offering is made. And in Acts 7:26, *synallassō*, "reconcile," refers to Moses attempting to solve a dispute between two brothers. Fitzgerald, "Paul and Paradigm Shifts," 241–42.

and humanity, and one (1 Cor. 7:11) is in reference to a relationship between spouses. Consequently, more traditional writings focus on Paul's use of the term *reconciliation* as it refers to the relationship between God and humanity. Although I begin with the relationship between God and humans, I also move toward a more interpersonal ethic. Indeed, although Christian reconciliation is rooted in the saving act of God, who reconciles Godself with humanity through Jesus, the concept of reconciliation has assumed a far more central place in Christian theology and society at large than might be expected from its limited use in the New Testament.

While the word *reconciliation* might mean different things depending on context, I use the term specifically to denote three types of reconciliation: (1) salvific, (2) social, and (3) civil. The first two types, salvific and social, are Christ-centered and grounded in trinitarian theology. Although the third type, civil, stems from Paul's letters, it is primarily secular in scope. Civil reconciliation, which emphasizes the diversity of human beings, is deeply rooted in the notion that all people have equal value. This ethic is exemplified by the ethnic and gender diversity of the contemporary Black Lives Matter movement—which, despite the adjective "Black," actually upholds the deeply egalitarian concept that all humans should be valued equally in American society.

The social and egalitarian ethic Paul addresses in Galatians 3:26–28 and 1 Corinthians 11:17–22 is often the basis for the continued popular use of the term *reconciliation* in both political and ecclesial contexts. I therefore begin by defining the three types of reconciliation I discuss, establishing their parameters of focus, and detailing what I call a biblical "trajectory of reconciliation," beginning with Peter's leadership and progressing into Paul's theology. After I move through this biblical foundation, I turn to the Civil Rights Movement and governmental attempts to foster reconciliation through institutions like affirmative action and legislation such as the Voting Rights Act of 1965. My trajectory of reconciliation then moves from the 1950s and 1960s, as a contextualized illustration, in arguing for the importance of human diversity across the whole of American society. First, however, I contextualize my three uses of the term.

Salvific Reconciliation

With the image of the Christian cross as a symbolic guide, we begin with salvific reconciliation. Salvific reconciliation is not so different from what one might hear described in church as atonement (or *at-one-ment*) with God. For this book's purpose, however, I use the term *salvific reconciliation*. Indeed, Paul describes reconciliation through the lens of those redeemed: "If anyone is in Christ, there is a new creation: everything old has passed away; see, everything has become new!" (2 Cor. 5:17). Accordingly, this first type of reconciliation is represented by the cross's vertical plane, representing humans being reconciled to God.

Figure I

The Two Planes of the Christian Cross

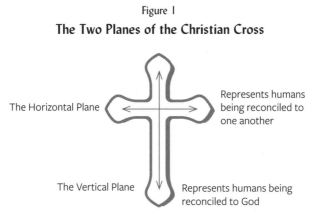

The Horizontal Plane — Represents humans being reconciled to one another

The Vertical Plane — Represents humans being reconciled to God

Paul writes in Romans, "For if while we were enemies, we were reconciled to God through the death of his Son, much more surely, having been reconciled, will we be saved by his life. But more than that, we even boast in God through our Lord Jesus Christ, through whom we have now received reconciliation" (5:10–11). Christians believe that, by his death and resurrection, Jesus broke through the boundaries of the world so that humans might be freed. Jesus's death liberated the world and restored humanity's relationship with God—meaning once more, humans became one with God. Salvific reconciliation then leads to social reconciliation: following in Jesus's leadership, we too are called to be reconcilers. Stated otherwise, as

Toni Morrison shared, "The function of freedom is to free somebody else."[5]

Social Reconciliation

Social reconciliation is based on salvific reconciliation but moves toward a political ethic rooted in an egalitarianism, or at least equal treatment of others, as found in Paul's letters. Victor Furnish argues that reconciliation is a binding thought in Paul's correspondence, from both theological and anthropological perspectives.[6] Due to its theological *and* social importance, God's act of reconciliation in Christ has significant implications for a Christian's identity, as we are made ambassadors of reconciliation. Once reconciled to God through Christ, Christians must also work toward reconciliation in the world.

Social Reconciliation Requires Equal Treatment of Others

Directly flowing from salvific reconciliation, social reconciliation asks, "Now that the human soul is saved, so what? How do humans relate to one another?" This places a compelling onus on humans to be more Christlike in their social treatment of one another because of the way God treated humans in reconciling them to Godself. In other words, if there is no social ethic attached to reconciliation, there is the danger of a "superficial discipleship that separates salvation from social transformation."[7] By focusing on Galatians 3:26–28, 1 Corinthians 11:17–22, and Romans 5–8, I will show that Paul addresses social issues in uniting Jews and gentiles—people of different origins, identities, and backgrounds—to transcend the boundaries of their differences so they can live together in community under an egalitarian social ethic.

Whereas salvific reconciliation relates to humans being reconciled to God *through Jesus*, social reconciliation relates to humans being reconciled to one another *because of Jesus*. In Paul's correspondence to the Galatians, for example, while rejecting arguments that gentile

5. Toni Morrison, commencement address at Barnard College, 1979.
6. See the summary in Victor Paul Furnish, "The Ministry of Reconciliation," *Currents in Theology and Mission* 4 (1977): 204–18.
7. Emmanuel Katongole and Chris Rice, *Reconciling All Things: A Christian Vision for Justice, Peace and Healing* (Downers Grove, IL: IVP Books, 2008), 28.

converts to Christianity must first undergo the Jewish custom of circumcision before becoming Christian, Paul emphasizes the uniform nature of salvation through Jesus and how human beings are equal to one another because of Jesus. "There is no longer Jew or Greek, there is no longer slave or free, there is no longer male or female; for all are one in Christ Jesus" (Gal. 3:28).

In *Christ and Reconciliation*, Veli-Matti Kärkkäinen speaks to the heart of the ethic defining social reconciliation by elaborating on this dynamic of equality in interpersonal relationships because of Christ. "The remarkable statement in Galatians 3:28 of the racial (Jews and Gentiles), societal (free and slave), and sexual (female and male) one[ness] in Christ is but the culmination of the great narrative of atonement and reconciliation that begins from the crucified Christ . . . and moves to . . . unite Jews and Gentiles."[8] Paul's Galatian correspondence provides a definitive biblical basis for arguing that racism, classism, and sexism are wrong. In order for the church to engage in social reconciliation, therefore, its members must treat all people as equals.

Social Reconciliation Requires Forgiveness for Previous Transgressions

In light of the history of how some dominant groups have oppressed and marginalized others—much in the way whites have oppressed Blacks or males have subjugated females—true social reconciliation can come about only with forgiveness. Just as God forgave humans *through Jesus*, reconciliation requires that humans forgive one another *because of Jesus*. In *Liberation and Reconciliation*, J. Deotis Roberts illustrates this by writing, "Forgiveness and reconciliation come to sinful humanity through the incarnation, which includes the cross and the resurrection. . . . Knowing the measure of God's love expressed in God's redemptive act in Christ should humble the Christian and enable one to love and forgive."[9] Stated otherwise,

8. Veli-Matti Kärkkäinen, *Christ and Reconciliation: A Constructive Christian Theology for the Pluralistic World* (Grand Rapids: Eerdmans, 2013), 1:367.

9. J. Deotis Roberts, *Liberation and Reconciliation: A Black Theology*, 2nd ed. (Louisville: Westminster John Knox, 2005), 62–63.

social reconciliation requires that human beings forgive one another, just as God forgives humans.

In addressing aspects of forgiveness while specifically detailing issues of power, L. Gregory Jones writes, "The practice of reconciling forgiveness calls us to unlearn the language that confuses, dominates, and controls and learn the 'redemptive language' that enables us to sustain community. Issues of forgiveness and reconciliation invariably involve issues of power."[10] Desmond Tutu contextualizes the necessity of forgiveness, especially with respect to imbalanced relationships, by detailing some of the atrocities revealed during the South African Truth and Reconciliation Commission hearings. He emphasizes the power of forgiveness by describing the magnanimity of those who forgave their tormentors and oppressors with an unprecedented generosity of spirit.[11] In *No Future without Forgiveness*, he describes Nelson Mandela's transition in South Africa from prisoner (under apartheid, from 1962 to 1990) to president (under democracy, in 1994). Mandela demonstrated his willingness to forgive by notably inviting his white former jailer to his inauguration as an honored guest. Tutu states, "He [Mandela] would be a potent agent for the reconciliation he would urge his compatriots to work for and which would form part of the Truth and Reconciliation Commission he was going to appoint to deal with our country's past. This man, who had been . . . incarcerated for nearly three decades, would soon be transformed into the embodiment of forgiveness and reconciliation."[12]

Mandela's witness provides a powerful example of how central forgiveness is in reconciliation. It also illustrates a truth that can be difficult to accept—that marginalized groups in the United States must, in the name of Christ, forgive those who have marginalized them if the country is ever really going to move toward reconciliation. Yet Jones is correct: "We cannot think about forgiveness without remembering horrifying evil: slavery in the United States, genocide

10. L. Gregory Jones, *Embodying Forgiveness: A Theological Analysis* (Grand Rapids: Eerdmans, 1995), 190.

11. Desmond Tutu, *No Future without Forgiveness* (New York: Doubleday Books, 1999), 144.

12. Tutu, *No Future without Forgiveness*, 10. See also Michael Battle, *Reconciliation: The Ubuntu Theology of Desmond Tutu* (Cleveland: Pilgrim Press, 1997), 10.

in Rwanda, the Holocaust in Nazi Germany."[13] As a Black man, a member of an oppressed minority group in America, I most certainly recognize the difficulty of unconditional forgiveness.

In reading *More than Equals: Racial Healing for the Sake of the Gospel*, I am encouraged by the perspective of Spencer Perkins, another Black man, who adopts a new perspective on grace, connecting God's unconditional forgiveness with our opportunity to be Christlike by extending forgiveness to others: "What's new about grace, at least for me, is that because we are grateful for what God did for us, we allow him to do the same to others through us. This means that if I know this loving God who is so full of grace, then I will forgive and embrace those who, like me, don't deserve my grace and forgiveness."[14] This includes forgiving and embracing even those who have played a part in America's ugly history of white supremacy.

From Mandela's example, in South Africa, and from the example of Martin Luther King Jr. (as we will see in chap. 3), it is clear that forgiveness is at the crux of social reconciliation. While the work of social reconciliation requires practical steps to *repair* our broken relationships and social spaces—in this country, through policy initiatives that include economic reparations, affirmative action, and the unfettering of voting rights—forgiveness remains fundamental to the very concept of reconciliation.

While the reconciliation paradigm requires reciprocal actions— forgiveness by the oppressed and a change in behavior by the oppressor— some argue that the oppressor has a duty also to repair, as much as possible, the damage caused. In other words, the oppressor has a duty to pursue reparations. I agree. In fact, the argument for reparations is supported by Scripture.[15] Luke's Gospel shares that after Zacchaeus acknowledged how he oppressed Jews, he promised to repair the damage his acts of oppression caused (19:8). Further, I believe (as James Forman of SNCC obviously believed in bringing

13. L. Gregory Jones and Célestin Musekura, *Forgiving as We've Been Forgiven: Community Practices for Making Peace* (Downers Grove, IL: IVP Books, 2010), 38.

14. Spencer Perkins and Chris Rice, *More than Equals: Racial Healing for the Sake of the Gospel*, Signature Edition (Downers Grove, IL: InterVarsity, 2021), 243.

15. See Jennifer Harvey, *Dear White Christians: For Those Still Longing for Racial Reconciliation*, 2nd. ed. (Grand Rapids: Eerdmans, 2020), xxiv.

the "Black Manifesto" to New York City's Riverside Church in 1969)[16] that reparations should be a part of the Christian responsibility. I am also of the opinion, however, that because of the proprietary nature of reparations, the federal government maintains culpability for acts of the past and the simultaneous capability to repair the damage done.[17]

Forgiveness, as Part of Social Reconciliation, Is a Ministry Jesus Left to the Church

In writing to the church in Corinth, Paul calls on members of the body of Christ not to count trespasses against one another but to be reconciled to one another, as God reconciled humanity to himself through Christ (2 Cor. 5:17–19). In expounding on Paul's reference and addressing the importance of forgiveness in reconciliation, Jones writes, "If we take scripture seriously, Christians have to acknowledge that we are not only a forgiven people called to forgive one another; we have also been entrusted with the message of God's forgiveness and reconciliation for the whole world."[18] Indeed, Jesus's ministry of forgiveness realizes itself in social reconciliation. It is in this regard that humans are ambassadors for Christ (2 Cor. 5:20).

While the vertical axis of the cross represents humans being reconciled to God, the horizontal axis represents reconciliation between humans and the creation of new egalitarian relationships (see fig. 1, page 20). Ralph Martin describes this divine legacy by arguing that reconciliation is more than a theological code word for God's work in restoring humanity in relation to God. In using Pauline congregations as an example, Martin explains that Christians must continue God's work of reconciliation with the entire world: "As Christians loved one another, forgave and were compassionate to one another, and showed forth in their mutual attitudes that they shared a new spirit which was not self-centered, hard-hearted or spiteful but one

---

16. Duke L. Kwon and Gregory Thompson, *Reparations: A Christian Call for Repentance and Repair* (Grand Rapids: Brazos, 2021), 97–98.

17. Williams A. Darity Jr. and A. Kirsten Mullen, *From Here to Equality: Reparations for Black Americans in the Twenty-First Century* (Chapel Hill: University of North Carolina Press, 2020).

18. Jones and Musekura, *Forgiving as We've Been Forgiven*, 38. See also Khobnya, "Reconciliation Must Prevail," 131.

that made for unity and harmony, so they were giving expression to the authenticity of the message of reconciliation."[19] As I show later in this chapter, the ministry of reconciliation is demonstrated by examples of social reconciliation in Scripture—in particular, we see this in Peter's leadership and Paul's theology.

Civil Reconciliation

Civil reconciliation—unlike salvific reconciliation and social reconciliation—is *not* necessarily Christian, or even religious. Instead, it is rooted in a moral ethic that seeks, among other things, governmental redress to remedy injustices. Civil reconciliation, for example, is at the heart of the Black Lives Matter movement. The application of a Pauline-inspired social reconciliation became contextualized as civil reconciliation during the Civil Rights Movement. The resistance, civil disobedience, and dissident fights for human equality that defined the ministry of Martin Luther King Jr. are examples of work toward civil reconciliation—just as is the contemporary work of ministers like the Reverend Dr. William J. Barber II and secular activists like Alicia Garza, Patrisse Cullors, and Opal Tometi (leaders of the Black Lives Matter movement).

Both social reconciliation and moral law influenced King's ministry and work in civil reconciliation. For example, in his famous "Letter from Birmingham City Jail," responding to the criticisms of his fellow clergy members regarding his secular engagement and resistance to human laws, King writes, "You express a great deal of anxiety over our willingness to break laws. This is certainly a legitimate concern. Since we so diligently urge people to obey the Supreme Court's decision of 1954 outlawing segregation in public schools, it is rather paradoxical to find us consciously breaking laws. One may well ask, 'How can you advocate breaking some laws and obeying others?' The answer is found in the fact that there are two types of laws: there are *just* and there are *unjust* laws. I would agree with St. Augustine that 'an unjust law is no law at all.'"[20]

19. Martin, *Reconciliation*, 230.
20. Martin Luther King Jr., "Letter from Birmingham City Jail," in *A Testament of Hope: The Essential Writings and Speeches of Martin Luther King, Jr.*, ed. James M. Washington (New York: HarperOne, 1996), 293 (emphasis in original).

Although not directly related to Christianity, civil reconciliation stems from a biblically based theological ethic that is rooted in an equal treatment of others. It is therefore an extension of social reconciliation insofar as people of faith, along with those outside the church who similarly subscribe to systems of fairness and equity, apply their notions of equality to political systems and structures beyond the church.

Civil reconciliation also takes Pauline theology, as exemplified in Galatians 3:26–28, and applies its intrinsic ethical value of "diversity in oneness" to political measures such as affirmative action and the Voting Rights Act of 1965 in order to support diversity and inclusion practices in society at large. Indeed, as Emmanuel Katongole and Chris Rice write in *Reconciling All Things*, "Promoting diversity just makes good business sense. Reconciliation becomes synonymous with celebrating differences or with making institutions and societies more 'inclusive' of diverse people groups."[21]

Further, as US Supreme Court Associate Justice Lewis Powell writes in *Regents of the University of California v. Bakke* (1978), the seminal decision upholding diversity considerations in higher education, "It is not too much to say that the 'nation's future depends upon leaders trained through wide exposure' to the ideas and mores of students as diverse as this Nation of many peoples."[22] Following the Supreme Court's logic, civil reconciliation presents an opportunity for the church's theology to benefit the secular world and for the diversity experiences of the secular world to benefit the church.

Peter's Leadership in Moving the Church toward Reconciliation: The Original Use of the Word *Church*

The word *church* (*ekklēsia*) is first used in the Bible in Matthew 16 and is a starting point for social reconciliation. It is used only twice

21. Katongole and Rice, *Reconciling All Things*, 29.
22. Regents of the University of California v. Bakke, 438 U.S. 256, 313 (1978). Diversity consultant Howard Ross also writes, "Educational institutions know that a diverse student body creates a better scholastic experience for their learners and that the quality of teaching improves when teachers demonstrate more inclusivity and less bias." *Everyday Bias: Identifying and Navigating Unconscious Judgments in Our Daily Lives* (Lanham, MD: Rowman & Littlefield, 2014), xii–xiii.

in all four Gospels, both times in Matthew (16:18; 18:17), and in both occurrences it means "assembly" or "gathering." *Ekklēsia* implies diversity. Note how Jesus, an itinerant *Jewish* preacher, originally used the term while conversing with Peter, his *Jewish* disciple, as they entered Caesarea Philippi, a predominantly *gentile* area (16:13). In one of the Bible's most popular quotations, Jesus approves of Peter's faithfulness and confession that Jesus is the foretold Jewish Messiah by exclaiming, "Flesh and blood has not revealed this to you, but my Father in heaven. And I tell you, you are Peter, and on this rock I will build my church" (16:17–18).

That first use of the word *church*, indicating an assembly or gathering of people, supports the conclusion that Jesus's intention has nothing to do with building a physical structure. Instead, his reference is to Peter's faith. Indeed, it comes just before he calls Peter "the rock" (*petros*) upon which he will build the *ekklēsia*—and the context implies that Jesus intends for the church to be an ethnically diverse group of people.

The Keys Are Symbols of Both History and Hope

During a visit to the Vatican, I stood in St. Peter's Square and saw the larger-than-life marble statutes of Saints Peter and Paul to the left and right, respectively, of the main entrance of the basilica. Directly atop the entrance is a detailed carving of Peter, kneeling in a posture of submission while surrounded by Jesus's other disciples. As Jesus stands above Peter, Jesus gives Peter *two* keys. One might ask, "Why *two* keys?" The Scripture clearly uses the plural (Matt. 16:19). But why two? Why not three or four?

The two keys symbolize two things: (1) Israel's history and (2) Israel's future. With the implicit reference to Isaiah 51:1–2 ("on this rock"), the first symbolic key that Jesus gives Peter represents Israel's history, a common theme in Matthew. Because of Peter's evidenced faith, however, the second key symbolizes Israel's future and the unique responsibility Jesus bestows on Peter to build the *ekklēsia*.

Underscoring an Old Testament connection, the symbolic keys of access to the church are reminiscent of the key of the house of David (Isa. 22:22), the same genealogical lineage from which Jesus descends (Matt. 1:6). As Matthew uniquely details Jesus giving Peter a key of legacy, representing Israel's history as God's chosen people, the narrative also details Jesus giving Peter a key of responsibility, representing Israel's future. As I will show in this chapter, the church's future includes it becoming a reconciling assembly, embracing both Jews and gentiles, the same way the contemporary church should reject xenophobia and embrace all people.

Matthew 16, with its setting in Caesarea Philippi, a place associated more with gentiles than with Jews, serves as a major turning point in Matthew's Gospel. It broadens the church's future invitation to include gentiles, in addition to Jews, while simultaneously connecting Jesus with the prophesies of Israel's past. It also includes elements unique to Matthew in its linking of Israel's history with her hopes.[23] Accordingly, Peter's confession is a bridge between Old Testament prophetic predications and Jesus, who is the fulfillment of the messianic Scriptures (see, e.g., 2 Sam. 7:12–13, 16). Arguably, therefore, Matthew's bridge-like nature—connecting the messianic Scriptures to Jesus as the foretold Messiah—is the reason for Matthew's primacy in the New Testament.

From Matthew 16's northern setting in Galilee, there is a physical transition as Jesus begins moving south toward Jerusalem (Matt. 16:21). There is also a shift in theological focus, as Matthew's version of Peter's confession appears to be more concerned with Peter and the *ekklēsia* than it is with Jesus. In fact, by this point Matthew has already broached the question of Jesus's identity (see, e.g., 11:3; 12:23). In chapter 14, after seeing Jesus walk on water, the disciples confess Jesus's lordship as "the Son of God" (14:33). Presumably, then, the confession in chapter 16 is less focused on telling readers who Jesus is (the Messiah) and more focused on telling them something about Peter's understanding and about Jesus's charge to Peter to build the church (16:19).

The Key of Legacy Representing Israel's History

In response to Jesus's question "Who do people say that the Son of Man is?" (Matt. 16:13), the disciples answer John the Baptist,

23. Donald Senior, *The Gospel of Matthew* (Nashville: Abingdon, 1997), 88.

Elijah, or Jeremiah (16:14). Matthew's inclusion of Jeremiah emphasizes the parallels he draws between Jesus and Jeremiah, a prominent prophet in Israel's history (2:17; 27:9). Moreover, in addition
to citing Jeremiah, Matthew includes Peter's confession that Jesus
is "the son of the living God" (16:16; cf. Mark 8:29; Luke 9:20),
again making a connection to the Old Testament (see Ps. 42:2) and
using a title with strong messianic overtones. Further, with respect
to Israel's history, Jesus lauds Peter and identifies him as "son of
Jonah" (Matt. 16:17). Either Jesus uses "Jonah" as a variant of
John (John 1:42), or Matthew is making yet another Old Testament
connection, this time between Peter's prophetic gifts and those of
Jonah.

The Key of Responsibility Representing Israel's Future

Matthew then shifts, looking ahead toward Israel's hopes by focusing on the anticipated building of the church. Jesus identifies
Peter as "the rock" and promises that upon that rock he will build
the church (Matt. 16:18), a designation subsequently used to specifically reference the assembly of believers (18:17). Moreover, before
Jesus mentions the keys, as symbols of authority, he declares that the
gates of Hades (the Greek god of the underworld) will not prevail
against the church (16:18). Jesus's gift to Peter reveals the path for
Israel's future as an inclusive community of both Jews and gentiles,
with authority to admit those formerly excluded symbolized by the
keys (16:19).

Expounding on the concept that the keys are a point of access to
the church, Donald Senior reminds us that the Matthew 16 narrative
is based on the story in Isaiah 22:15–25, in which Eliakim is given the
key to the house of David and the key's power is to open and shut the
gates. "Peter is invested as the master of the household of Jesus and
given the power to 'bind and loose' (16:19); his decision will be ratified by heavenly authority. The terms 'binding and loosing' are used in
rabbinic literature to cover several functions, including the authority to
determine membership, to impose rules and sanctions, and even for the
power of exorcism. The same power is given to the community itself
in 18:18 where the issue at stake is clearly the authority to determine

membership."[24] Insofar as the keys represent authority, I believe Jesus's reference to "binding" and "loosing" denotes a practical interpretation of his teachings and how members of the community forgive one another as members of the church (Matt. 18:15–18; see also John 20:23). To return to social reconciliation, this means that humans—both inside and outside the church—must learn to forgive one another.

The Church Was Born as a *Jewish* Assembly

Following the Bible's canonical sequence, Jesus entrusting Peter with Israel's past and future—with determining who will receive admission to the church—"the assembly" (i.e., the church) officially comes into being on the day of Pentecost, when Peter preaches and a diverse group of people are admitted to the church. Acts 2 describes a diverse *ekklēsia*, a bringing to fruition of the anticipated church that Jesus previously described (Matt. 16:18).

In addressing such diversity of identity within Judaism, Aaron Kuecker writes, "The initial group of Jesus-followers are identified by the crowd as 'Galileans,' implying both the salience of Galilean identity and differentiation between Galileans and the subgroup identities within the crowd."[25] It is therefore apparent that on the day of

24. Senior, *Gospel of Matthew*, 191–92. Furthermore, regarding membership in the church and laying a foundation for a trajectory of reconciliation, I believe it is important to juxtapose Paul's implications for Jews and Jewish Christians as they relate to membership in the church. In writing to the Galatians, Paul addresses a dispute between Jewish Christians and gentile Christians over whether gentile Christians must first conform to the Mosaic covenant, including circumcision, before accepting Christ. After emphatically rejecting such arguments, Paul writes in the letter's benediction, "For neither circumcision nor uncircumcision is anything; but a new creation is everything! As for those who will follow this rule—peace be upon them, and mercy, and upon the Israel of God" (Gal. 6:15–16). Susan Grove Eastman does an excellent job in arguing that, as a Jew, Paul, with his benediction, does not forget his fellow Jews who *will not* become members of the church. She argues that "Israel continues to exist in the present tense, distinct from the church, as the object of God's providence, judgment, and mercy. As such, in Gal. 6:16 Israel is a sign of God's commitment to history, to flesh and blood people, beyond as well as within the confines of the church." "Israel and the Mercy of God: A Re-reading of Galatians 6:16 and Romans 9–11," *New Testament Studies* 56 (2010): 95.

25. Aaron J. Kuecker, *The Spirit and the "Other": Social Identity, Ethnicity and Intergroup Reconciliation in Luke-Acts* (London: T&T Clark, 2011), 112.

Pentecost, a diversity of subgroups formed the church, originally with "Other" Jews (Acts 2:9–11). Will Willimon reminds us, however, that God's works are proclaimed *only* to Jews at this point, because the time is not yet ripe for the divisions between Jews and gentiles to be healed. Instead, "in Peter's speech we are listening to a Jew speaking to fellow Jews; linking the story of Jesus with the Scriptures of the Jews."[26] Returning to the Matthean analogy of the keys, Acts 2 unlocks only the past. It is not until Acts 10 that Peter begins to unlock hope for the church's future. True reconciliation, therefore, occurs when gentiles join the church *with Jews*.

Reconciliation under Peter's Leadership: The Church Admits Gentiles as "the Other"

Acts 10 describes how the church engages in reconciliation, overcoming the boundaries of religion and race, when the *Jewish* Peter baptizes the *gentile* Cornelius. In noting this event's overall significance in moving the church toward reconciliation, Kuecker states, "Indeed, Luke is concerned with the notions that 'Gentiles' could participate in salvation history . . . , that non-Israelites could retain ethnic particularity and even that non-Israelites and Israelites could engage in fellowship with one another. But Luke's appreciation of these factors both stems from and, in practice, requires a clear reality: that all who identify with Jesus are incorporated into a group *sharing a common identity* that affirms yet transcends ethnic identity."[27] Accordingly, Acts 10 speaks to both salvific *and* social reconciliation, recognizing that one of the church's core ethics is equality.

The narrative begins with Peter praying on a rooftop and receiving a strange vision of various animals descending, animals he is commanded to kill and eat (Acts 10:13). In refusing to do so, stating

26. William H. Willimon, *Acts*, Interpretation, a Bible Commentary for Teaching and Preaching (Atlanta: John Knox, 1998), 35.

27. Kuecker, *The Spirit and the "Other,"* 182. The Acts 10 narrative does not discount the significance of Acts 8, where Phillip baptizes Simon the Samaritan (8:12–13) and the unnamed Ethiopian eunuch (8:36–38). The eunuch was presumably gentile, as he could not have been a Jew or a proselyte to Judaism (Lev. 21:20; Deut. 23:1).

that he has never eaten anything profane or unclean (10:14), Peter responds with a strict adherence to Jewish dietary laws. But he is told, "What God has made clean, you must not call profane" (10:15). This scenario occurs twice more before Peter is moved to action (10:16).

Peter's initial resistance, presumably shaped by his background as an observant Jew, betrays his unconscious bias against those who are not members of his ethnic community. This ethnic boundary was so powerful that it took divine intervention to defeat Peter's xenophobia and convince him that those he had previously treated as "Others" should now be welcome members of God's people too. In *Fear of the Other*, Willimon writes about this type of bias: "Xenophobic, exclusionary fear of the Other is more than a matter of preference for people whom we enjoy hanging out with. . . . We separate ourselves from others . . . whom we have judged to be so Other as to be beyond the bounds of having any bond between us."[28] Peter's divinely inspired move past his unconscious bias led to reconciliation. Indeed, divine inspiration is still needed, as unconscious bias and racism continue to plague society.

In exemplifying both inclusiveness and social reconciliation, Peter states, "I truly understand that God shows no partiality, but in every nation anyone who fears him and does what is right is acceptable to him" (Acts 10:34–35). In commenting on the central importance of these verses and noting the Lukan motif of a progression toward inclusiveness, Robert O'Toole argues, "Luke's theme of the mission to the Gentiles represents social advance. No longer does one have to belong to a given people or observe all the details of the Torah (cf. Acts 15:28–29) to be saved. Luke summarizes his position in Peter's statement, 'Truly, I perceive that God shows no partiality, but in every nation anyone who fears him and does what is right is acceptable to him' (Acts 10:34–35). God gives the Gentiles the same gift he gave to those at Pentecost (Acts 11:17)."[29]

28. William H. Willimon, *Fear of the Other: No Fear in Love* (Nashville: Abingdon, 2016), 7.
29. Robert F. O'Toole, "Luke's Position on Politics and Society in Luke-Acts," in *Political Issues in Luke-Acts*, ed. Richard J. Cassidy and Phillip J. Scharper (Maryknoll, NY: Orbis Books, 1983), 10.

From a soteriological perspective, O'Toole's commentary speaks to salvific reconciliation. More to my point, however, from an egalitarian perspective, salvific reconciliation lies at the very heart of social reconciliation. Regardless of ethnicity, sexual orientation, economic background, or geography, social reconciliation means that *all people* are equal within the *ekklēsia*.

TWO

SOCIAL RECONCILIATION

Paul's Theology of Equality in Christ Jesus

Paul's Theology in Moving the Church toward Reconciliation

In chapter 1, I detailed a biblical trajectory of reconciliation by exploring select Scripture passages that revealed Peter's leadership in moving the *ekklēsia* toward inclusiveness, culminating with the Acts 10 narrative, in which Peter baptizes Cornelius, the first gentile recorded as becoming a member of the church. In building on this foundation, I now connect Peter's leadership to Paul's theology by exploring the church's egalitarian-like move toward equitable social relations. I specifically focus on Paul's theology of equality—the very heart of social reconciliation. I provide a historical contextualization of social reconciliation using three select examples from Paul's authentic letters as well as an overview of Paul's underlying theology.[1] This discussion will lay a foundation for the concept of civil reconciliation—the practical implementation of Paul's social reconciliation and the basis for understanding the Black church's work during the Civil Rights Movement, which is the focus of the next chapter.

---

1. As previously highlighted, I support the view that only seven of the New Testament's thirteen writings attributed to Paul are authentic. In canonical order, they are Romans, 1 Corinthians, 2 Corinthians, Galatians, Philippians, 1 Thessalonians, and Philemon. See Victor Paul Furnish, *The Moral Teaching of Paul: Selected Issues*, 3rd ed. (Nashville: Abingdon, 2009), 11–12.

There are arguably no better examples of social reconciliation in Paul's writings than (1) the most popular and frequently cited part of Galatians (3:26–28), (2) the portion of the Corinthian correspondence dealing with abuses of the Lord's Supper (1 Cor. 11:17–22), and (3) the four chapters from Romans that emphasize equality in Christ from both a theological and an ethical perspective (Rom. 5–8). Before exploring these scriptural examples, however, we turn to Paul's background to consider how it influenced his theology.

Paul's Background and Uniqueness

Paul is unique among biblical figures. Along with Jesus and Peter, Paul is one of the most influential people in the New Testament. Over one-half of Luke's narrative in the book of Acts is dedicated to Paul's career, from his time as a persecutor of the church to his imprisonment and ministry in Rome. Moreover, thirteen New Testament letters, composing the Pauline corpus, were traditionally attributed to Paul.[2] It is no wonder, therefore, that Paul is such a towering figure in the history of Christian thought.

To understand social reconciliation in Paul's writings, I believe it is beneficial to examine Paul himself as readers of the Bible meet him in Acts and in the limited autobiographical information Paul provides. My intention is to provide an overview of Paul's background insofar as it sheds light on his theology of equality.

Before His Conversion, Paul Was a Hellenized Diaspora Jew and a Persecutor of the Church

Scripture is silent as to when Paul was born. Although Paul's letters do not reference his place of birth, Acts indicates that he was born in Tarsus (Acts 21:39; 22:3). Since it is apparent from Paul's letters

2. In addition to the seven authentic epistles cited in note 1 of this chapter, six other letters are considered "deutero-Pauline"; although they bear Paul's name, their authenticity is greatly disputed. The six letters in canonical order are Ephesians, Colossians, 2 Thessalonians, 1 Timothy, 2 Timothy, and Titus. As Furnish highlights, "Ordinarily, scholars attribute these six disputed letters to at least four writers and date them (variously) to the decades following Paul's death, from as early as the 70s to as late as the first decade of the second century." *Moral Teaching of Paul*, 12.

that he knew Greek as a native language and that he was well skilled in interacting with both Jews and gentiles (see, e.g., 1 Cor. 9:19–23), it is likely that Paul was from the diaspora (Jews living outside of Palestine), which included Jews in Tarsus.[3] In considering biographical details of Paul's life in Acts as well as Paul's own references in his epistles, Ralph Martin writes, "Saul of Tarsus began his religious life and career as a Pharisee, that is, as an adherent to a religious way of understanding and doing the will of Israel's God."[4]

Acts indicates that Paul's father was Jewish, that Paul was a member of the Jewish sect of the Pharisees, and that he was the son of Pharisees (Acts 23:6). In regard to Paul's background and heritage: "He boasts from time to time in his letters of his Jewish past in rebuttal to other missionaries who caused problems in the churches that he had founded (see Phil. 3 and 2 Cor. 11). Paul reveals that prior to being a Christian he was a zealous Pharisee."[5] Presumably, therefore, Paul's Pharisaic ideology and love for traditional Judaism caused him to become a persecutor of the church in Judea before his conversion to what we now know as Christianity.

Acts describes Paul's preconversion zeal at the stoning of Stephen and his persecution of the church (Acts 7:58–8:3). In fact, in Galatians, Paul writes of being keenly aware of how his reputation preceded him and how it might be an impediment to his ministry: "Then I went into the regions of Syria and Cilicia, and I was still unknown by sight to the churches of Judea that are in Christ; they only heard it said, 'The one who formerly was persecuting us is now proclaiming the faith he once tried to destroy'" (Gal. 1:21–23). Further, with respect to how Paul's reputation preceded him, Acts, in describing Paul's famous conversion narrative, details Ananias's fear in response to a divine directive to minister to Paul: "But Ananias answered, 'Lord, I have heard from many about this man, how much evil he has done to your saints in Jerusalem'" (Acts 9:13).

3. Paul J. Achtemeier, Joel B. Green, and Marianne Meye Thompson, *Introducing the New Testament: Its Literature and Theology* (Grand Rapids: Eerdmans, 2001), 289.

4. Ralph P. Martin, *Reconciliation: A Study of Paul's Theology* (Grand Rapids: Academie Books, 1989), 9.

5. Marion L. Soards, *The Apostle Paul: An Introduction to His Writings and Teaching* (New York: Paulist Press, 1987), 19.

In *Social-Science Commentary on Letters of Paul*, Bruce Malina and John Pilch elaborate on Paul's background as influencing his zealous persecution of the church by highlighting his Israelite heritage and his Pharisaic style of living the Mosaic Torah. They write that "in terms of the values embodied by Pharisaic ideology, his zeal moved him to become a 'persecutor of the church,' that is, of the members of the Jesus group he encountered in Judea."[6] This persecution took place before Paul's conversion (Acts 9:3–19; 22:4–16; 26:9–18), before Paul came to believe that the God of Israel had called him to be an Israelite prophet and to proclaim the gospel to Israelites and non-Israelites.

Although Paul was from the tribe of Benjamin (Phil. 3.5), he was a hellenized diaspora Jew. In arguing that Paul's Hellenistic background influenced his gospel proclamation, Calvin Roetzel writes,

> Paul's early years were spent in Tarsus, a center of Stoic teaching. Although his letters show signs of Stoic influence (e.g., his use of the diatribe), Paul's outlook differs markedly from that of his Stoic contemporaries. His gospel is fundamentally historical; it is rooted in a historical event, based on a historical person, anticipates a fulfillment in the historical (real) future. Unlike the Stoic view of freedom as spiritual autonomy, freedom for Paul means liberation from hostile powers (death, sin, etc.) for service to Christ. The Stoic is confident man can win freedom through his own efforts; Paul sees freedom as the result of action by God. And whereas the Stoic's concern centers on freedom, and thus on the individual, *Christianity, says Paul, concerns life, and thus the interaction of men* [and women].[7]

Roetzel implies that Paul's theology of freedom directly pertains to human beings' ability to interact with one another on an equal basis. This is not only the core of social reconciliation, but it also became a foundational theology that buttressed the Black church's prophetic resistance during the Civil Rights Movement.

6. Bruce J. Malina and John J. Pilch, *Social-Science Commentary on Letters of Paul* (Minneapolis: Fortress, 2006), 10.

7. Calvin J. Roetzel, *The Letters of Paul: Conversations in Context*, 2nd ed. (Atlanta: John Knox, 1982), 22 (emphasis added).

Paul's Experiences Underscore His Theology

According to the book of Acts, after Paul's conversion experience (9:1–19), he began to proclaim Jesus as the foretold Messiah (9:20–22). But Victor Furnish writes, "Even after his call to apostleship, Paul's faith and thought continued to be shaped by the Jewish Scriptures, although he read them now from the standpoint of his new life in Christ."[8] So although Paul became a Christian, in that he was clearly a follower of Jesus the Christ, his continued allegiance to aspects of Pharisaic Judaism demonstrates that he also maintained his Jewish heritage.

Indeed, well after Paul's apostolic call in Acts 9, he cited his Judaism while on trial for, among other things, promulgating a belief in the resurrection. Acts records Paul openly proclaiming his Jewish heritage: "When Paul noticed that some were Sadducees and others were Pharisees, he called out in the council, 'Brothers, I am a Pharisee, a son of Pharisees'" (Acts 23:6). Just as all of Paul's theology was influenced by his background and his experience of Jesus, the Messiah sent by the God of Israel, so his theology of equality resulted from both his Pharisaic past and his personal encounter with the resurrected Christ.

Paul's Theology Is about Equitable Relations and Liberation

Although Paul clearly writes from an eschatological perspective, anticipating the second coming of Christ, the "*parousia*" (see, e.g., Rom. 13:11–12; 1 Cor. 15:51–52; 1 Thess. 4:13–17), his theology is about equitable social relations as much as or arguably more than anything having to do with salvation or the afterlife. Consistent with this, Margaret Mitchell describes 1 Corinthians as an argument for ecclesial unity based on its statement "I urge you, brothers and sisters, through the name of our Lord Jesus Christ, to all say the same thing, and to not let there be factions among you, but to be reconciled in the same mind and in the same opinion" (1:10, trans. Mitchell).[9] But in a

---

8. Furnish, *Moral Teaching of Paul*, 57.

9. Margaret M. Mitchell, *Paul and the Rhetoric of Reconciliation: An Exegetical Investigation of the Language and Composition of 1 Corinthians* (Louisville: Westminster John Knox, 1991), 1.

situation of oppression, equitable social relations (and with them true unity and reconciliation) can be achieved only through liberation.

In *No Longer Slaves*, Brad Braxton explores Paul's liberationist perspective, basing his argument on Paul's experience and championing Paul's gospel of freedom. Braxton argues, "Paul offers to the Gentile Galatian converts (and to other groups that have been marginalized) the criterion of experience as the basis for acceptance by God. In the case of the Galatians, it is the experience of faith that was confirmed by the activity of the Holy Spirit. In fact, Paul may value the role of experience highly because it was an experience that transformed him into the apostle of the Gentiles."[10]

Following Braxton's logic, just as Paul's conversion experience was the basis for his liberation, the experiences of others, and their faith as predicated on those experiences, are the basis for their liberation too. Although America's caste system and her Jim Crow laws subjugated Blacks in the American South, King led the Black church in a liberationist movement because of the special freedom Black Christians found in Paul's theology of equality—a theology that affirmed their experience of being, despite what the unjust laws and bigoted whites might say, truly equal. On the basis of their God-given equality, they fought for equitable social relations (which is to say, true unity and reconciliation).

This theme of social unity and equality *because of Jesus* is consistent as an undergirding focus of the selected texts from Galatians (3:26–28), the Corinthian correspondence (1 Cor. 11:17–22), and Romans (Rom. 5–8).

Social Reconciliation in Galatians, 1 Corinthians, and Romans

In chapter 1, I distinguished between salvific and social reconciliation. Whereas salvific reconciliation involves humans being reconciled to God *through Jesus*, social reconciliation involves humans being reconciled to one another *because of Jesus*. In Paul's authentic letters,

---

10. Brad R. Braxton, *No Longer Slaves: Galatians and African American Experience* (Collegeville, MN: Liturgical Press, 2002), 57.

social reconciliation is exemplified in an egalitarian-like ethic calling for equitable relationships in the *ekklēsia*. In building on the previously set foundation of Paul's background and theology, and moving toward an understanding of social reconciliation, I argue that Paul's thinking was shaped not only by his Jewish heritage and, of course, his conversion experience but also by his experiences with the currents of the Greco-Roman world.[11]

Some of the sociopolitical and cultural trends that Paul experienced came to bear on his writings. For example, "as an apostle to the Gentiles, Paul encouraged his congregations not only to continue to participate, as good citizens, in the life of the city, but also to behave in a manner that would bring approval from the outsiders."[12] These "outsiders" are the proverbial "Others" with whom Paul sought equitable relations, as revealed in Galatians (Gal. 3:26–28), the Corinthian correspondence (1 Cor. 11:17–22), and Romans (Rom. 5–8).

Social Reconciliation in Galatians: Paul's Most Definitive Statement on Equality because of Jesus

As a matter of organization, although these categories are not rigid or exclusive, Galatians can be divided into three sections: (1) history (chaps. 1–2), (2) theology (chaps. 3–4), and (3) ethics (chaps. 5–6).[13] Braxton notes that the categories overlap, indicating, "One should not treat each section as separate, but as constituent parts of Paul's overall defense of his gospel of freedom."[14] Because the underlying focus of this chapter is theological, my primary concern in contextualizing the Galatian correspondence is the second section, chapters 3–4, wherein Paul frequently references Old Testament texts, which he views as pointing to the Christ-event and the inclusion of non-Jews.

In commenting on Paul's theology in Galatians, Charles Cousar writes, "The theological excitement of Galatians lies in the radical interpretation Paul makes of the meaning of God's grace. It is more

11. Furnish, *Moral Teaching of Paul*, 66.
12. Corneliu Constantineanu, *The Social Significance of Reconciliation in Paul's Theology: Narrative Readings in Romans* (London: T&T Clark, 2010), 50–51.
13. Braxton, *No Longer Slaves*, 56–57.
14. Braxton, *No Longer Slaves*, 57.

than a doctrine; it is an experience. At the same time, it is *the* doctrine which undergirds all that Paul fights for in this letter."[15] The theological focus of Galatians, and the letter's central theme, is freedom. Nancy Bedford expounds on freedom's significance in Galatians by distinguishing the type of freedom at issue. She writes, "It is not the freedom to consume or dominate but the freedom to love and to be transformed even more in God's image and likeness."[16] Social reconciliation requires the responsible use of freedom as a means to love and accept others as equal because of Jesus.

Galatians 3:26–28 is Paul's most definitive theological account of social equality. Indeed, this is arguably the most pronounced statement on equitable relations in the entire New Testament. While rebuking the teachings of other itinerant preachers—teachings he felt were inconsistent with a theology of equality in Christ—Paul writes to the fledgling church, "For in Christ Jesus you are all children of God through faith. As many of you as were baptized into Christ have clothed yourselves with Christ. There is no longer Jew or Greek, there is no longer slave or free, there is no longer male and female; for all of you are one in Christ Jesus" (Gal. 3:26–28). Seeing no need for gentiles to convert to Judaism before becoming Christian, Paul obviously affirms that membership in the church is open to both Jews and gentiles alike.

Most interpreters believe that Paul is quoting here from a baptismal liturgy used in his and other Christian congregations and also that the same theology is present in Romans 10:12, 1 Corinthians 12:13, and Colossians 3:11. Furnish writes on the social aspect of this Galatians passage, highlighting that "within its original liturgical setting, it was addressed to newly baptized persons, declaring them to have been transferred into a believing community that participates in a wholly new order of existence. They now inhabit a realm in which their lives are no longer defined by the religious, gender, and social distinctions they had previously taken for granted."[17]

15. Charles B. Cousar, *Galatians* (Louisville: Westminster John Knox, 2012), 8 (emphasis in original).
16. Nancy Elizabeth Bedford, *Galatians* (Louisville: Westminster John Knox, 2016), 11.
17. Furnish, *Moral Teaching of Paul*, 106–7.

This undergirding theology, presumably adopted in a baptismal liturgy but also cited by Paul in support of equality in the church, is the crux of social reconciliation. Both in its original usage and in the Galatian correspondence, this baptismal confession suggests that through Christ old racial and cultural divisions are healed. In other words, Paul is saying that it is a fundamental tenet of Christianity that humans are not only reconciled to God *through Jesus*; they are also equal with one another *because of Jesus*.

Paul seemingly recognizes that baptism into the *ekklēsia* minimizes ethnic, social, and gender distinctions—although they remain present. With respect to Paul's baptismal liturgy of equal welcome into the *ekklēsia*, Braxton argues, "The confession focuses on three spheres that were and are notorious hotbeds of social strife: *ethnic relationships* ('there is neither Jew nor Greek'), *social class* ('there is neither slave nor free'), and *gender relationships* ('there is neither male and female'). Paul is cognizant of the importance of all three spheres in fostering social harmony in the church."[18]

Stated otherwise, social reconciliation, as found in Galatians 3, means that all humans are reconciled to one another because all people are equal in the body of Christ. But equal does not mean the same. Baptism is supposed to bring diverse people into a diverse church.

Bedford reflects on the Galatians 3 passage by sharing, "Different people with diverse ethnicities, social status, and genders are invited to relate in new ways in Christ. They are not forced into sameness; to be equal does not mean to be identical."[19] On this point about theological equality and diversity in the church, Braxton states, "Paul's entire evangelistic campaign was designed to bring the Gentiles into the church as Gentiles. In other words, Paul preached a law-free gospel among the Gentiles in order to ensure ethnic diversity in the Church."[20]

---

18. Braxton, *No Longer Slaves*, 93 (emphasis in original). Moreover, in considering the overall context of the Galatian correspondence and the issues that necessitated Paul writing it, Braxton also argues, "In Galatians 3 . . . he focuses primarily on the first, namely ethnic relationships. One could argue that the establishment of a proper relationship between Jews and Gentiles who are 'in Christ Jesus' is the central challenge that precipitates the writing of the entire letter" (93).

19. Bedford, *Galatians*, 97–98.

20. Braxton, *No Longer Slaves*, 94.

Indeed, Paul's call for unity did not seek to abolish ethnic and gender differences; rather, Paul sought to appreciate them.[21]

According to Braxton, "When Paul says, 'There is neither Jew nor Greek, there is neither slave nor free, there is neither male and female,' he is not asserting the obliteration of difference, but rather the obliteration of *dominance*."[22] Obliterating dominance means eliminating ethnic, social, and class divisions along with the hierarchal social practices that were common in the Greco-Roman world. If differences remain but *dominances* are obliterated, the *ekklēsia* Jesus builds on Peter's faith (Matt. 16:13–19) will be a socially diverse place where *all* people are treated equally because of their common entry through baptism and their common faith: "For in Christ Jesus you are all children of God through faith" (Gal. 3:26). In revisiting the Acts 10 example from chapter 1, when the Jewish Peter baptized the gentile Cornelius, the two were no longer separated by a relationship of social or ethnic dominance. Instead, as Peter came to realize, "God shows no partiality, but in every nation anyone who fears him and does what is right is acceptable to him" (Acts 10:34–35).

Paul's theology of equality is the basis for social reconciliation because *all* members of the church are one in Christ Jesus (Gal. 3:28). This foundational belief in "oneness" was the theological basis for the Black church's acts of resistance and work toward reconciliation during the Civil Rights Movement. In advocating for a culture of diversity and inclusion, Paul truly illustrates the heart of social reconciliation.

Social Reconciliation in 1 Corinthians: "Do This in Remembrance of Me"

It is clear in 1 Corinthians that Paul's motivation for writing is at least twofold. There had been an oral report from "Chloe's people" (presumably members of a house church meeting at Chloe's residence) informing Paul about divisions among the Corinthian believers (1 Cor. 1:11). Paul had also apparently received a letter from a delegation that raised issues about morality (7:1). From the report he

21. Braxton, *No Longer Slaves*, 94.
22. Braxton, *No Longer Slaves*, 94 (emphasis in original).

received from Chloe's people, Paul learned that social factions among members of the church were caused by special affections people had for the minister who had baptized them (e.g., Paul, Apollos, or Cephas). They did not recognize the commonality they shared with one another because of baptism into the *ekklēsia* (3:3–23). It is, at least in part, because of this type of pronounced social division that Paul wrote the Corinthian correspondence. Another division that Paul addresses involved the Corinthians' hierarchical social practices, which came out in their observance (and abuse) of the Lord's Supper. The Corinthian correspondence makes clear that these practices conflicted with Paul's vision of communal unity in Jesus's name.

Richard Hays explains that the Corinthians' observance of the Lord's Supper had nothing to do with the sacramental rites that are customary in church liturgies today. Instead, he notes, the observation of the Lord's Supper in the Corinthian context was literally a common meal that was shared in community at a private home.[23] In following the caste system typical in the Greco-Roman world, however, the Corinthians allowed more privileged members of the community to receive more and better food than the less privileged members. Stated otherwise, wealthy Christians in Corinth ate better than poor Christians.

Paul was unequivocal in expressing his disdain for such social practices. He wrote to the church, "For when the time comes to eat, each of you goes ahead with your own supper, and one goes hungry and another becomes drunk. What! Do you not have homes to eat and drink in? Or do you show contempt for the church of God and humiliate those who have nothing? What should I say to you? Should I commend you? In this matter I do not commend you!" (1 Cor. 11:21–22). In reflecting on this passage, Roetzel notes, "Some celebrated the Lord's Supper as if it were the Great Messianic Banquet reserved for the end of time. In their enthusiasm, they stuffed themselves, saving nothing for Christian slaves whose arrival was delayed by assigned tasks. Some were gorged and drunken; not a crumb remained for others."[24] This class-based practice was the very antithesis of social reconciliation.

23. See Richard B. Hays, *First Corinthians* (Louisville: Westminster John Knox, 2011), 193.

24. Roetzel, *Letters of Paul*, 56.

In addressing the obvious social divisions among the Corinthians, Hays also writes, "Paul regards this as a humiliation of the community and an abuse of the Supper of the Lord, whose own example contradicts such status divisions."[25] According to Paul's theology of equality, the Corinthians should have embodied unity in their remembrance of Jesus through the Lord's Supper.

Social Reconciliation in Romans: An Ethical Implication of Paul's Theology of Salvation

The passages from Galatians and 1 Corinthians contextualized an egalitarian ethic of social reconciliation based on equality in the church. This third example, Romans 5–8, again emphasizes social equality. As highlighted in chapter 1, the *ekklēsia* is a diverse body composed of people of different ethnicities (Acts 10:34–35). It also includes people from different socioeconomic backgrounds (1 Cor. 11:21–22). In Romans 5–8, we see how Paul addresses members of the church from different ethnic backgrounds.

Each of Paul's undisputed letters deals with a specific situation, and Romans is no exception. Paul wrote Romans, probably from Corinth around the mid-50s, to a mixed audience of Jewish and gentile believers in an attempt to bring various ethnicities into a reconciled relationship with one another. Indeed, the main issue Paul addresses is the disunity between Jews and gentiles.

The central subject of the book of Romans is God's grace in re-establishing God's lordship over humanity. This is based on faith instead of ethnicity. Paul Achtemeier states, "Faith, or trust (both translate the same Greek word) is the mode by which that lordship is accepted. The fact that the relationship of gracious lordship between Creator and creation is now based on faith, rather than on race (as it was in the case of the Jews as chosen people), means the relationship has now been universalized to extend beyond the bounds of the Jewish race."[26]

In providing what is arguably the letter's thesis, Paul states, "For I am not ashamed of the gospel; it is the power of God for salvation to everyone who has faith, to the Jew first and also to the Greek.

---

25. Hays, *First Corinthians*, 194.
26. Paul J. Achtemeier, *Romans* (Louisville: Westminster John Knox, 2010), 20–21.

For in it the righteousness of God is revealed through faith for faith; as it is written, 'The one who is righteous will live by faith'" (Rom. 1:16–17). Social reconciliation is one of the most important themes in Romans, and Paul develops it as an explication of the inner logic of God's gospel of righteousness and as an appropriate response to Rome's ethnic disunity.

Sociopolitical events in Rome most certainly led to the ethnic divisions Paul addresses in the letter. Corneliu Constantineanu writes, "That Christianity in Rome began around Jewish synagogues explains its initial Jewish pattern of thought and behavior. The increasing number of Christians from among the Jews gave rise to frequent disturbances and conflicts between Jewish Christians and the Jews, which contributed substantially to the expulsion of the Jews and Jewish Christians from Rome, through Claudius' edict, most probably around AD 49."[27] Due to Claudius's edict (Acts 18:2), the Roman churches were left with a predominant and growing gentile population that likely distanced itself from the church's Jewish population.

By the time Paul wrote Romans, urban Roman Christianity was separated from the federation of synagogues, and "when the Jewish Christians began to return to Rome around the mid-50s, they found a completely new situation, with the Gentile Christians in leadership positions and a life marked by non-Jewish patterns of religious life as well as a diminished emphasis on key Jewish convictions and practices."[28] These were the fractured ethnic divisions Paul had to address. His ethical treatment of "the Other" and leading a new life in Christ through baptism (Rom. 6:4) are at the core of Paul's theology of equality in Romans.

Paul lays out an interconnected relationship between salvific and social reconciliation, making the latter the logical consequence of the former while addressing social relations between Jewish Christians and gentile Christians living in Rome. For Paul, social reconciliation along racial lines is a moral imperative that stems from salvific reconciliation as a way of extending obedience to Christ.

As stated earlier, there is a "vertical" plane representing humans being reconciled to God (salvific) and a "horizontal" plane representing

---

27. Constantineanu, *Social Significance of Reconciliation*, 101.
28. Constantineanu, *Social Significance of Reconciliation*, 101–2.

humans being reconciled to one another (social) (see fig. 1 on p. 20). Constantineanu interprets Paul's theology in Romans as bringing the two planes together as inseparable and interconnected parts. "Paul's presentation of reconciliation contains an essential horizontal/social dimension. I argue that beginning with Romans 5.1, Paul uses interchangeably different metaphors and symbols of salvation such as 'justification' (vertical category) and 'peace,' 'love,' 'reconciliation,' (horizontal, relational categories), in order to express the inseparability of the two aspects of reconciliation."[29] Paul indeed sees social reconciliation among different peoples as an integral part of living out the ministry of salvific reconciliation.[30]

In his book *One Blood*, John Perkins addresses this same connection between salvation and the equitable treatment of others. In arguing that the church has a divine mandate for reconciliation and that people in the church are supposed to set the example of treating others equally, because the church (*ekklēsia*) is rooted in the gospel, Perkins writes, "For too long, many in the Church have argued that unity in the body of Christ across ethnic and class lines is a separate issue from the gospel. There has been the suggestion that we can be reconciled to God without being reconciled to our brothers and sisters in Christ. Scripture doesn't bear that out."[31] Perkins is correct.

The vertical and horizontal planes, symbolizing salvation and equitable social relations, are interconnected through baptism into the church. Paul describes the consequence of human salvation as an ethic that demands baptized members of the church treat one another equally, regardless of their differences. "Therefore we have been buried with him by baptism into death, so that, just as Christ was raised from the dead by the glory of the Father, so we too might walk in a newness of life" (Rom. 6:4). This statement connects salvific and social reconciliation in Romans.

In addressing an ethical response to Paul's call for reconciliation in chapter 5 (Rom. 5:10–11), insofar as (salvific) reconciliation stems from baptism, Ben Witherington III describes Romans 6:4 by writing, "Paul

29. Constantineanu, *Social Significance of Reconciliation*, 99.
30. Constantineanu, *Social Significance of Reconciliation*, 99.
31. John M. Perkins, *One Blood: Parting Words to the Church on Race and Love* (Chicago: Moody, 2018), 32.

indicates that through baptism the believer is buried with Christ 'into death.' Death is not seen here as an event, as we speak of the time of death, but rather as a state which one enters."[32] In this regard, baptism correlates with burial and death, as opposed to the resurrection, since humans have yet to experience the resurrection—a state of perfection in which humans will be conformed to Jesus's state of being.[33] In describing a newness of *the current life* (as opposed to of the afterlife), verse 4 moves reconciliation from the eschatological into the social realm.

In again drawing on the imagery of the cross, with respect to the ethical and social implication of salvation, Paul doesn't accept simply a vertical or legal transaction between God and humanity. Paul embraces a process that necessarily involves a moral transformation in the lives of believers.

Whereas salvific reconciliation places sinful humans in right relationship with God *through Jesus*, and social reconciliation requires that humans treat one another equally *because of Jesus*, Paul's underlying argument in Romans 5–8 is that, because humans have been reconciled to God, baptism into the church imposes an ethical obligation to treat others as equals, regardless of their ethnic or socioeconomic status, by leading a new life. This is the very core of social reconciliation, and it directly derives from salvific reconciliation.

Constantineanu states, "Paul used the reconciliation language to bring about unity and mutual acceptance among the believers in Rome and . . . the rhetoric of reconciliation was important for the entire argument of Romans."[34] This argument is most certainly at the heart of chapters 5–8.

Applying Social Reconciliation's Threefold Criteria to Paul's Theology of Equality

In chapter 1, while connecting but simultaneously distinguishing salvific and social reconciliation, I argued that social reconciliation requires three things: (1) equal treatment of others, (2) forgiveness

32. Ben Witherington III, with Darlene Hyatt, *Paul's Letter to the Romans: A Socio-Rhetorical Commentary* (Grand Rapids: Eerdmans, 2004), 158.
33. Witherington III, *Paul's Letter to the Romans*, 158.
34. Constantineanu, *Social Significance of Reconciliation*, 99.

for previous transgressions, and (3) a recognition that forgiveness is a part of the ministry of reconciliation that Jesus left to the church. I now apply these criteria to the biblical texts just discussed. The third criterion will connect this discussion to the next chapter's account of civil reconciliation, the practical implementation of social reconciliation.

Equal Treatment of Others

Each of the three selected biblical texts emphasizes an egalitarian-like treatment of others. In Galatians 3, Paul provides what is arguably the New Testament's most pronounced explanation of equality. With freedom as an undergirding basis of the letter, Paul promotes a freedom to love and accept "the Other" as one would want to be loved and accepted. In what was probably a baptismal liturgy, Galatians 3:26–28 speaks to ethnic, social, and gender equality because of Jesus. Similarly, the 1 Corinthians passage calls for equal treatment of others regardless of socioeconomic standing or class. Although Romans 5–8 is anchored in salvific reconciliation (5:10–11), it also has to do with equal treatment of others—based largely on racial, ethnic, and socioeconomic dynamics—after emphasizing an ethically imposed social response to the unity established in baptism (6:4).

Forgiveness for Previous Transgressions

Although not an explicit focus, forgiveness for previous transgressions is unquestionably implied in all three of the texts. In Galatians, forgiveness for previous sins is implied using a twofold perspective. First, from a gender perspective, "Paul assures the Galatians in [chapter 3] verse 26 that through the faith of Jesus Christ they are all children of God . . . inasmuch as all have the full rights that only male heirs received in that context."[35] This implies that those who have been subjugated should forgive those who did the subjugating. Second, from a social perspective, as Paul emphasizes the equitable treatment of others, "clothing" oneself with Christ (Gal. 3:27) implies forgiving others, as we "wear the garb of forgiveness and new

35. Bedford, *Galatians*, 91.

life that Christ embodies for us."[36] In addressing this point, Joseph Liechty writes, "Reconciling involves the complementary dynamics of repenting *and* forgiving, the first a way of dealing with having done wrong, the second with having suffered wrong. Thus reconciliation is achieved when perpetrators have repented and victims have forgiven."[37] Galatians implicitly calls for both repentance and forgiveness in its emphasis on equitable treatment and communal relations among all people as equals.

The passage from 1 Corinthians also implies forgiveness (and repentance) as it envisions an ongoing and interactive relationship among people of various socioeconomic backgrounds meeting together for a common meal. Authentic interaction and sharing in such a space are possible only if forgiveness is both given and received. Further, baptism—as emphasized in Romans—requires people to forgive and repent, and to thereby move toward reconciliation. Past transgressions must be forgiven, just as changed behavior is expected.

A Recognition That Forgiveness Is a Part of the Ministry of Reconciliation That Jesus Left to the Church

Paul's second surviving letter to the church at Corinth provides a scriptural point of reference for forgiveness: "So if anyone is in Christ, there is a new creation: everything old has passed away; see, everything has become new! All this is from God, who reconciled us to himself through Christ, and has given us the ministry of reconciliation; that is, in Christ God was reconciling the world to himself, not counting their trespasses against them, and entrusting the message of reconciliation to us" (2 Cor. 5:17–19). This passage speaks to both salvific *and* social reconciliation (with an emphasis on forgiveness), while also connecting the two with civil reconciliation.

As in legal succession, where heirs inherit as descendants of family members who predecease them, members of the church are the spiritual heirs of Jesus. The Galatians passage, with its implications

---

36. Bedford, *Galatians*, 92.

37. Joseph Liechty, "Putting Forgiveness in Its Place: The Dynamics of Reconciliation," in *Explorations in Reconciliation: New Directions in Theology*, ed. David Tombs and Joseph Liechty (Burlington, VT: Ashgate, 2006), 60 (emphasis added).

for forgiveness, expressly concludes with a reference to intergenerational (and interreligious) spiritual heirship, connecting the children of Israel to the *ekklēsia* by referencing Abraham—the progenitor of Christianity, Islam, and Judaism: "And if you belong to Christ, then you are Abraham's offspring, heirs according to the promise" (Gal. 3:29). Further, complementing the 1 Corinthians passage on equality during the Lord's Supper (11:17–22), Paul adds in 2 Corinthians, "If anyone is in Christ, there is a new creation: everything old has passed away; see, everything has become new!" (5:17)—implying that social divisions of rich and poor, or "haves" and "have nots," become immaterial within the church. Reconciliation is about restoring broken relationships (including those broken by social hierarchy), as social hierarchy becomes irrelevant within the church.

Finally, along with the evisceration of social divisions by the grace we have all received equally through Christ (Rom. 5:17), Paul speaks of salvation, noting that God has reconciled us humans to Godself, not counting our trespasses against us but entrusting the message of reconciliation to us (2 Cor. 5:18–19). In *Forgiving As We've Been Forgiven*, L. Gregory Jones reflects on this connection and writes, "If we take Scripture seriously, Christians have to acknowledge that we are not only a forgiven people called to forgive one another; we have also been entrusted with the message of God's forgiveness and reconciliation for the whole world."[38] In other words, because God forgave human transgressions *through Jesus*, humans are likewise entrusted with a ministry of reconciliation *because of Jesus* and are consequently called to forgive one another. This is part of the ministry Jesus left to the church—to us, his spiritual heirs.

---

38. L. Gregory Jones and Célestin Musekura, *Forgiving As We've Been Forgiven: Community Practices for Making Peace* (Downers Grove, IL: IVP Books, 2010), 38.

THREE

CIVIL RECONCILIATION

Contextualizing King and the Black Church's
Ministry of Reconciliation

Civil Reconciliation Stems from Social Reconciliation

The previous chapter explored social reconciliation in Paul's letters by examining his theology of equality in response to specific situations that prompted him to write portions of Galatians, 1 Corinthians, and Romans. I concluded by pairing three specific criteria of social reconciliation with these passages, arguing that social reconciliation requires (1) equal treatment of others, (2) forgiveness for previous transgressions, and (3) a recognition that forgiveness is a part of the ministry of reconciliation that Jesus left to the church.

Forgiveness is a part of the ministry of reconciliation that Jesus left to the church, and civil reconciliation—a practical outgrowth of social reconciliation—is a ministry encompassing forgiveness as the church interfaces with the secular world. This is particularly important in considering the current context of the diverse and multiethnic activists who compose the Black Lives Matter movement, as marginalized groups and their allies have again come together to oppose social subjection. Insofar as reconciliation is ongoing, especially as clergy leaders engage in secular politics within the prophetic domain of ministry, the divisive issues moving the contemporary church to reconciling action are similar to the issues that moved her to engage in civil reconciliation during the Civil Rights Movement. Forgiveness is still a critical part of the conversation.

The division between Christians (and between their respective denominations, for that matter) over engaging in or staying out of secular politics is well documented.[1] History suggests, however, that it is not surprising that the Black church, under Martin Luther King Jr.'s leadership, led the entry of the church into the Civil Rights Movement. In *The Black Church in the Post–Civil Rights Era*, Anthony Pinn documents the Black church's entry into secular politics: "It was not until the civil rights movement that there developed a persistent and collective cooperation on national issues of injustice and discrimination. Through participation in this push for social transformation and political change, black leaders and their churches came full circle. . . . The Black Church also provided the ideological and theological underpinning for the movement."[2]

Indeed, the goal of the Black church, as it relates to her engagement in politics, was the pursuit of liberation, justice, and reconciliation by seeking good for *all people*, especially those who had been marginalized, through the politics of resistance.[3] As Henry Louis Gates Jr. writes, "Rooted in the fundamental belief in equality between Black and white, . . . the Black Church and the religion practiced within its embrace acted as the engine driving social transformation in America."[4] With a focus on King's leadership, I argue that there is a sociopolitical parallel between the Black church's historic entry

1. An excellent historical exploration of whether Christians are called to be engaged in or refrain from political activity is woven throughout H. Richard Niebuhr, *Christ and Culture*, 50th ann. ed. (New York: HarperOne, 2001). Further, with respect to the ongoing conflict within Black church communities, in *The Divided Mind of the Black Church: Theology, Piety, and Public Witness* (New York: New York University Press, 2014), 53–61, Raphael Warnock chronicles a tension between pietistic and liberationist strands that was arguably best illustrated by the initial resistance to King's liberationist theology. See also C. Eric Lincoln and Lawrence H. Mamiya, *The Black Church in the African American Experience* (Durham, NC: Duke University Press, 1990), 212–13.

2. Anthony B. Pinn, *The Black Church in the Post–Civil Rights Era* (Maryknoll, NY: Orbis Books, 2002), 13.

3. Amy E. Black, "Introduction: Christian Traditions and Political Engagement," in *Five Views on the Church and Politics*, ed. Amy E. Black and Stanley N. Gundry (Grand Rapids: Zondervan, 2015), 13.

4. Henry Louis Gates Jr., *The Black Church: This Is Our Story, This Is Our Song* (New York: Penguin, 2021), 4.

into the secular political affairs of the Civil Rights Movement and more contemporary denominational responses to the "Make America Great Again" political narrative, connected by the common thread of forgiveness.

Although "Make America Great Again" (MAGA) is widely connected to Donald Trump's 2016 presidential campaign and his volatile one-term presidency, my use of the expression is much broader. In the next chapter, I will discuss how Trump's race-based rhetoric unearthed great discord among people, showing that acrimony, racial enmity, and xenophobia are as prevalent in contemporary society as they were at any point in American history, including the era of the Civil Rights Movement. These divisions did not go away when Trump left the White House. In fact, I would argue that the infamous January 6, 2021, insurrection and attempted overthrow of the US Capitol was evidence of the MAGA enmity Trump left behind after leaving the presidency thirteen days later.

In comparing church political activism during the 1950s and '60s with the contemporary resurgence of church political activism brought on by the MAGA narrative, I suggest that issues in both time frames necessitated that the church respond to repressive governmental policies. Such prophetic responses are examples of civil reconciliation, of which forgiveness is a necessary element.

Although civil reconciliation addresses more than just ethnic divisions, King's leadership was largely centered on racial reconciliation—a need that most certainly still exists in both Christian and secular communities. By exploring King's leadership, this chapter shows how the Black church exemplified the ministry of forgiveness, through civil reconciliation, connecting it with secular politics as an embodiment of Paul's theology of equality.

This chapter begins with the end in mind, arguing that forgiveness is a critical element of reconciliation, before discussing King's leadership in the Black church as an exemplar of civil reconciliation. I also briefly examine the Black church's historical tension between pietistic theology and political activism, while providing an overview of the theology King embraced to undergird the Civil Rights Movement—a theology heavily based on Paul's writings on equitable social relations.

The Importance of Forgiveness in Civil Reconciliation

In describing reconciliation, Richard Lischer writes, "Reconciliation looks different in innumerable contexts—different in South Africa than in the United States, different in inter-Christian dialogue than in Christian-Muslim dialogue, different at a conference table than at a kitchen table."[5] In arguing that the church's role in reconciliation includes society at large, I build on the previous chapter's contextualization of Paul's theology of equality by examining the Black church and her political activism; in following Lischer's logic, I argue that civil reconciliation looks like the church entering the secular realm while simultaneously engaging in a ministry of forgiveness.

As noted in the previous chapter, forgiveness is a part of the ministry of reconciliation that Jesus left to the church. Lischer posits that "God's work of reconciliation is acknowledged when each person accepts God's forgiveness in Jesus Christ and embraces the fullness of his or her humanity."[6] Following Lischer, humans are reconciled to God *because of Jesus* and also eschatologically reconciled with one another. This theological truth calls humanity to the ministry of reconciliation in the present age—a ministry that includes both God's forgiveness of us and our forgiveness of one another. I agree with Brenda Salter McNeil: "Reconciliation is an ongoing spiritual process involving forgiveness, repentance and justice that restores broken relationships and systems to reflect God's original intention for all creation to flourish."[7] L. Gregory Jones actually connects forgiveness to God's original intention for creation, in *Embodying Forgiveness.* He writes, "A Christian account of forgiveness ought not simply or even primarily be focused on the absolution of guilt; rather, it ought to be focused on reconciliation of brokenness, the restoration of communion—with God, with one another, and with the whole Creation. Indeed . . . Christian

5. Richard Lischer, *The End of Words: The Language of Reconciliation in a Culture of Violence* (Grand Rapids: Eerdmans, 2005), 134.

6. Lischer, *End of Words,* 137.

7. Brenda Salter McNeil, *Roadmap to Reconciliation: Moving Communities into Unity, Wholeness, and Justice* (Downers Grove, IL: InterVarsity, 2015), 22.

forgiveness must be at once an expression of a commitment to a new way of life."[8] In also arguing that forgiveness is a sign of the peace of God's original creation, Jones's analysis is the embodiment of the previously cited Scripture from 2 Corinthians.[9]

Forgiveness can be a difficult practice, especially in certain imbalanced relationships. There were imbalanced relationships in the Greco-Roman world, where imperial Romans marginalized and persecuted Jews. There were imbalanced relationships during the Civil Rights Movement, when many white supremacists used Jim Crow laws to subjugate the Black community in the segregated South. More recently, there were also imbalanced relationships between George Floyd, Ahmaud Arbery, and Breonna Taylor and their respective killers. Despite these imbalances, however, a Christocentric perspective acknowledges that members of the church are called to love their enemies and that the church's practice of forgiveness makes things new. This "newness," as the consequence of forgiveness, was popularized by King in the Black church's struggle for civil reconciliation.

Contextualizing Civil Reconciliation

The Black Church's Entry into the Secular Politics of the Civil Rights Movement

There are different theories as to what event launched the Civil Rights Movement. Although some might argue it was the Supreme Court's decision in *Brown v. Board of Education* (1954), I argue that the December 1955 arrest of Rosa Parks—a very active member of St. Paul African Methodist Episcopal Church in Montgomery, Alabama—and the subsequent Montgomery Bus Boycott were its genesis.[10] In *The Black Church in the African American Experience*,

8. L. Gregory Jones, *Embodying Forgiveness: A Theological Analysis* (Grand Rapids: Eerdmans, 1995), xii.

9. Jones, *Embodying Forgiveness*, xii.

10. See Jonathan C. Augustine, "The Fiery Furnace, Civil Disobedience, and the Civil Rights Movement: A Biblical Exegesis on Daniel 3 and Letter from Birmingham Jail," *Richmond Public Interest Law Review* 21, no. 3 (2018): 243–62. See also Pinn, *Black Church in the Post–Civil Rights Era*, 13: "With Rosa Parks's arrest . . . a boycott was called for and the Baptist Ministerial Alliance in Montgomery responded by

C. Eric Lincoln and Lawrence Mamiya advance the former view while nevertheless holding up the bus boycott as a pivotal moment:

> The case which came to symbolize a decisive break with the past began when Rev. Oliver Leon Brown of the St. Mark's A.M.E. Church in To-peka, Kansas—supported by the NAACP Legal Defense Fund—sued the Board of Education on behalf of his nine-year-old daughter Linda Brown and all other black children similarly injured by segregation in the public schools. The resultant Supreme Court decision granting the relief requested set in motion the civil rights movement which reached its zenith under the leadership of Martin Luther King, Jr. . . . It was Dr. King who led the year-long . . . boycott . . . which culminated in a decisive defeat of segregation in the public transportation system of that one-time capital of the Confederacy.[11]

Regardless of exactly when the Civil Rights Movement began, the Montgomery Bus Boycott certainly introduced the world to King, then the pastor of Montgomery's Dexter Avenue Baptist Church.

My intent is not to elaborate extensively on King's background. Volumes have been dedicated to chronicling his life. I instead rely primarily on Lischer's *The Preacher King*[12] and Peter Paris's *Black Religious Leaders*[13] to help explain the Black church's entry into the secular politics of the Civil Rights Movement and consequently the work of civil reconciliation. King's Montgomery pastorate served as a crucible in which the social ethic of Paul's theology of equality confronted Jim Crow discrimination in the South.

After chronicling King's 1954 arrival in Montgomery and installation as pastor of Dexter Avenue, Lischer describes the Montgomery Bus Boycott in setting the course for the Black church's political engagement.[14] He notably describes the boycott's beginning, detailing King's election as president of the hastily formed Montgomery

---

becoming part of . . . the Montgomery Improvement Association. . . . The work of this organization . . . grew into a movement for civil rights across the United States."

11. Lincoln and Mamiya, *Black Church*, 211.

12. Richard Lischer, *The Preacher King: Martin Luther King, Jr. and the Word That Moved America* (New York: Oxford University Press, 1995).

13. Peter J. Paris, *Black Religious Leaders: Conflict in Unity* (Louisville: Westminster John Knox, 1991).

14. Lischer, *Preacher King*, 73–76.

Improvement Association, King's powerful oration at Holt Street Baptist Church—just over a year after his pastoral installation at Dexter Avenue—and the synthesis of ideas King forged as history was set in motion.

Describing King's preaching and the Black church's entry into politics, Lischer writes, "By means of a wealth of literary, biblical, and philosophical allusions, [King] assured his hearers that history and universal moral law are aligned with the black quest for freedom. . . . Like a priest, he mediated a covenant with which white moderates and liberals were comfortable. . . . He reinforced this commonality in many ways—with psychological jargon, popular religious sentiment, the grammar of inclusion, and by a synthesis of biblical and civil-religious rhetoric."[15]

King also addressed the issue of race in political oratory, likening the struggle of Blacks in the Jim Crow South to the struggle of oppressed Jews in the Old Testament. Lischer writes that "after the Boycott had commenced, King's Sunday morning sermons found a new purpose and vitality. The specificity of *race*, which he had assiduously avoided in his graduate education, now sharpened the point of his biblical interpretation and preaching."[16] Indeed, King's transformative oratory at Holt Street Baptist Church, in beginning the boycott, reminded America of the words of the prophet Amos, who similarly challenged governmental action twenty-eight centuries earlier: "But let justice roll down like waters, and righteousness like an ever-flowing stream" (Amos 5:24). As the Civil Rights Movement began, King's preaching became political and the Black church entered politics, institutionally beginning the work of civil reconciliation.

Piety or Politics: The Black Church Was Divided as to Whether It Should Play a Role in Civil Reconciliation

In the wake of the successful Montgomery Bus Boycott, King argued that the church must be engaged not only in spiritual matters but also in sociopolitical ones. In his first book, *Stride toward Freedom*, King wrote that "religion operates not only on the vertical plane

15. Lischer, *Preacher King*, 10–11.
16. Lischer, *Preacher King*, 85 (emphasis in original).

but also on the horizontal. . . . This means . . . it seeks to change the souls of men, and thereby unite them with God; . . . it [also] seeks to change . . . environmental conditions . . . so that the soul will have a chance after it is changed."[17] Having been reared in the social milieu of politically active Black clergy and having studied influential figures like Walter Rauschenbusch, King synthesized the gospel's concern for souls *and* society—a synthesis that fueled the Civil Rights Movement.

In *The Divided Mind of the Black Church*, Raphael Warnock points out that the foregoing synthesis—of the vertical and the horizontal, of concern for souls and for society—was a common rhetorical thread appearing throughout King's writings and oratory.[18] As Warnock makes plain, influenced by the social gospel movement, King sought civil reconciliation through the Black church's political engagement with the secular world by connecting a religion that focused on salvation in heaven with action that meets temporal needs on earth.[19] This applied theology, which moves religious conviction into social action, has been called "evangelical liberalism."[20] Insofar as it moves the church toward political action, it is arguably the essence of the church's work in civil reconciliation.

But not all Black leaders agreed with King and his desire for the Black church to play a role in civil reconciliation. The philosophy of evangelical liberalism—a progressive Christian movement that takes modern knowledge, science, and ethics into consideration while emphasizing the importance of individual reason and experience—was and is opposed by conservative evangelicalism, the philosophy exhibited by Black church leaders such as Joseph H. Jackson, the longest-serving president of the National Baptist Convention, USA,

17. Martin Luther King Jr., *Stride toward Freedom: The Montgomery Story* (Eugene, OR: Wipf & Stock, 2001), 36.
18. Warnock, *Divided Mind of the Black Church*, 43.
19. Warnock, *Divided Mind of the Black Church*, 43 (citing Martin Luther King Jr., "Why Jesus Called a Man a Fool," in *A Knock at Midnight: Inspiration from the Great Sermons of Martin Luther King, Jr.*, ed. Clayborne Carson and Peter Holloran [New York: Warner Books, 1998], 141–42).
20. Anthony E. Cook, "Beyond Critical Legal Studies: The Reconstructive Theology of Dr. Martin Luther King, Jr.," in *Critical Race Theory: The Key Writings That Formed the Movement*, ed. Kimberlé Crenshaw et al. (New York: New Press, 1995), 95.

Inc.[21] Jackson was a great patriot who believed in the goodness of America, even arguing, "The supreme law of the land, appropriately amended by due process, holds out a promise to Blacks that gradually has been honored and that will be more completely fulfilled in due time."[22] Jackson was against people taking the law into their own hands and setting the stage for "mob rule." Paris writes that "Jackson expended considerable energy during the '60s in admonishing civil rights workers not to employ similar methods. Rather, he preached that every citizen should have faith in the legal machinery of the nation and in the justice set forth so prominently in the federal Constitution."[23]

Jackson's philosophy on Black church leadership was indeed antithetical to King's. It was also presumably the reason for the famous 1961 split in the National Baptist Convention, USA, Inc., after King and other anti-Jackson forces staged a march-in at the convention. Jackson's leadership represented a non-emancipatory Black church faction that exemplified conservative evangelicalism and was clearly more interested in piety than protest politics.

The opposite is true of evangelical liberalism. Warnock highlights the Black church's liberationist nature and King's leadership in bringing her squarely into secular affairs:

> The view that privileges "the saving of souls," while ignoring or marginalizing the transformation of the social order as central to the soteriological message of the biblical witness and the essential mission of the church is clearly *inconsistent* with any doctrine of the church that can be derived from the radical side of the black church's witness. The liberationist thrust of black religion can be traced from slave religion to the freedom thrust of the independent black church movement to the ministry of Martin Luther King, Jr. The leader of the church-led movement for liberation, King and his SCLC challenged any narrow and individualistic understanding of the church's mission that focuses exclusively on "saving souls." Rather, King and those who served with him set out to "Redeem the Soul of America."[24]

21. Cook, "Beyond Critical Legal Studies," 91.
22. Paris, *Black Religious Leaders*, 76.
23. Paris, *Black Religious Leaders*, 76–77.
24. Warnock, *Divided Mind of the Black Church*, 137 (emphasis in original).

Although King's prophetic leadership formally brought the Black church, as an institution, into secular politics, the Black church was birthed in the politics of resistance and has always been engaged in such.[25]

Civil Reconciliation through the Resistance of Civil Disobedience

Almost ten years after writing *Stride toward Freedom*, King responded to the well-documented history of church leaders rebuking and resisting the church's engagement in secular politics. In 1963, after an act of civil disobedience that led to his arrest in Birmingham, King famously wrote "Letter from Birmingham City Jail" to squarely address fellow members of the clergy who criticized his leadership and to explain a crucial distinction: "There are *just* and there are *unjust* laws," he says; "I would agree with Saint Augustine that 'an unjust law is no law at all.'"[26] In elaborating on King's logic, Paris writes, "King had advocated time and again that those who acquiesce to evil participate in promoting evil and are, therefore, as much the agents of evil as the intimidators themselves."[27] King sought to be neither an agent of evil nor an oppressive intimidator. Instead, as someone molded by a "suffering servant theology" (including a belief

25. See Jonathan C. Augustine, "And When Does the Black Church Get Political? Responding in the Era of Trump and Making the Black Church Great Again," *Hastings Race & Poverty Law Journal* 17, no. 1 (2020): 87–132. The African Methodist Episcopal Church (AME Church) is the oldest connectionally operated Black Church in America. See Lincoln and Mamiya, *Black Church*, 51–52. The AME Church originates from a 1787 breakaway from what was then the Methodist Episcopal Church (the precursor to the United Methodist Church) in Philadelphia. African American worshipers formed the Free African Society, a precursor to the legal establishment of the AME Church, because they were treated in a discriminatory manner during worship. See Richard S. Newman, *Freedom's Prophet: Bishop Richard Allen, the AME Church, and the Black Founding Fathers* (New York: New York University Press, 2008), 173–76. Argument can therefore be made that the Black church has been involved in resistance politics since its inception in 1787.

26. Martin Luther King Jr., "Letter from Birmingham City Jail," in *A Testament of Hope: The Essential Writings and Speeches of Martin Luther King, Jr.*, ed. James M. Washington (New York: HarperOne, 1996), 293 (emphasis in original).

27. Paris, *Black Religious Leaders*, 120–21.

that suffering is redemptive),[28] King risked his life for civil reconciliation when he went to jail in Birmingham.

King's distinction between the two types of laws was an important basis for the civil disobedience that fueled his politics of resistance. He concluded that segregation laws were unjust because they degrade human personality and promote a false sense of inferiority.[29] As I see it, the very genesis of the Civil Rights Movement—Rosa Parks's refusal to move to the back of the bus in Montgomery—was the consequence of a suffering servant theology working with and through civil disobedience, an embodiment of the church's work toward civil reconciliation.

In *Walker v. City of Birmingham* (1967), the US Supreme Court records that in the days prior to King's arrest in Birmingham, he and other Black ministers applied for, but did not receive, a parade permit (which was required by municipal ordinance) for their protest against the city's discriminatory conditions.[30] The Alabama courts issued an injunction against the ministers, hoping to keep them from assembling anyway (i.e., without a permit), and the US Supreme Court affirmed the injunction. In doing so, the court did not consider the merits of the ministers' actions. Instead, it looked only at the fact that they assembled without a permit—concluding that, in light of the Alabama courts' injunction, the assembled ministers were, in fact, in contempt of court.

When King marched without a permit, disobeying what he deemed a morally "unjust law" and readily accepting incarceration as the consequence of his action, his theology was rooted in civil disobedience, but it was also biblically based. After his arrest and subsequent incarceration, King addressed the ongoing necessity for oppressed groups to engage in civil disobedience to take on their governmental oppressors. With a biblically based ethic, he referenced the prophetic

28. The Civil Rights Movement's suffering servant theology—paraphrased as redemptive hope through sacrificial suffering—is based on the messianic connection of Isaiah 53 to certain parts of the Gospels. See, e.g., William H. Bellinger Jr. and William R. Famer, eds., *Jesus and the Suffering Servant: Isaiah 53 and Christian Origins* (Harrisburg, PA: Trinity Press International, 1998). King documented his view of suffering as redemptive in an essay that was originally published in the *Christian Century* in 1960. It has been reproduced as "Suffering and Faith," in *Testament of Hope*, 41–42.

29. King, "Letter from Birmingham City Jail," 293.

30. Walker v. City of Birmingham, 388 U.S. 307 (1967).

resistance in Daniel 3: "Of course, there is nothing new about this kind of civil disobedience. It was seen sublimely in the refusal of Shadrach, Meshach and Abednego to obey the laws of Nebuchadnezzar because a higher moral law was involved. It was practiced superbly by the early Christians who were willing to face hungry lions and the excruciating pain of chopping blocks, before submitting to certain unjust laws of the Roman Empire."[31]

King was therefore proud to lead a movement that was a continuation of centuries-old prophetic political resistance. Such faith-based political engagement, which seeks governmental redress for those pushed to the margins of society, is part of the church's work toward civil reconciliation. It was also the very foundation of the way Jesus began his social justice ministry (Luke 4:18–19).

King's nonviolent leadership was greatly influenced by his study of Mohandas Gandhi's civil disobedience during the Indian Independence Movement of the 1940s.[32] Most important, however, insofar as King was a product of the church, was the influence of Jesus's unconditional love. In specifically addressing this foundational nexus of Christ and Gandhi, King writes,

> From the beginning a basic philosophy guided the movement. This guiding principle has since been referred to variously as nonviolent resistance, noncooperation, and passive resistance. But in the first days of the protest none of these expressions was mentioned; the phrase most often heard was "Christian love." It was the Sermon on the Mount, rather than a doctrine of passive resistance, that initially inspired the Negroes of Montgomery to dignified social action. It was Jesus of Nazareth that stirred the Negroes to protest with the creative weapon of love. . . . Nonviolent resistance had emerged as the technique of the movement, while love stood as the regulating ideal. In other words, Christ furnished the spirit and motivation while Gandhi furnished the method.[33]

31. King, "Letter from Birmingham City Jail," 294.

32. See Charles Marsh, *The Beloved Community: How Faith Shapes Social Justice, from the Civil Rights Movement to Today* (New York: Basic Books, 2005), 45–46. See also Yxta Maya Murray, "A Jurisprudence of Nonviolence," *Connecticut Public Interest Law Journal* 9, no. 1 (2009): 65–159.

33. Martin Luther King Jr., "The Violence of Desperate Men," in *The Autobiography of Martin Luther King, Jr.*, ed. Clayborne Carson (New York: Grand Central Publishing, 1998), 67.

A theologically based morality was indeed the impetus for Gandhi's use of civil disobedience in India as well as for King's use of civil disobedience in the Jim Crow South. King's position on civil disobedience literally set the tone for the church's work toward civil reconciliation for the entire Civil Rights Movement.

King's engagement in civil reconciliation was based on an ecclesiology that holds that the church should be involved in politics to bring about necessary social change. His leadership underscored the egalitarian themes Paul expresses in each of the three Scripture passages detailed in the previous chapter (1 Cor. 11:17–22; Gal. 3:26–28; and Rom. 5–8). King's theologically based ethic of taking on the secular world to advance a community rooted in equality is at the heart of civil reconciliation. Indeed, although there was and is still a dichotomy between dominant and marginalized groups, the Black church's work in civil reconciliation during the 1960s helped inaugurate a "civil version" of social reconciliation and of Paul's theology of equality.

Revisiting Forgiveness as a Part of Reconciliation: King's Theology with a More Contemporary and Applied Response

This chapter began by noting the importance of forgiveness in any genuine dialogue regarding reconciliation. In addressing the difficulty of forgiveness, Allan Boesak notes that regardless of how monstrous a deed another person may have committed, they are still a child of God, and all humans have sinned in grave enough fashion for God to disclaim us. He writes that "if reconciliation needs political forgiveness, reconciliation needs communal and personal forgiveness. For reconciliation to be genuine, we should allow ourselves to be subverted by the grace and mercy of God. Radical reconciliation requires less self-righteousness, less hypocrisy, less self-defensiveness, less judgmental arrogance."[34] Although not easy, genuine forgiveness—a

---

34. Allan Aubrey Boesak, "Subversive Piety: The Reradicalization of Desmond Tutu," in *Radical Reconciliation: Beyond Political Pietism and Christian Quietism*, ed. Allan Aubrey Boesak and Curtiss Paul DeYoung (Maryknoll, NY: Orbis Books, 2012), 148–49.

part of the ministry of reconciliation that Jesus left to the church (2 Cor. 5:17–19)—is required.

In *Liberation and Reconciliation*, J. Deotis Roberts similarly writes of the relationship between forgiveness and reconciliation—sharing that they come to us sinful humans through the incarnation, which includes the cross and resurrection. He shares that "grace is costly and is manifest only when there is an 'I-thou' encounter between us and God. Knowing the measure of God's love expressed in God's redemptive act in Christ should humble the Christian and engage one to love and forgive."[35] Love and forgiveness, and with them the ministry of reconciliation, were indeed hallmarks of King's ministry and of the Civil Rights Movement. And they have remained hallmarks of the Black church, as exemplified by some of the responses to the June 2015 racially motivated shooting at Mother Emanuel AME Church in Charleston, South Carolina—in which, after a Bible study, the young Dylann Roof opened fire, killing nine people.[36]

Jesus taught about the love that is required for genuine reconciliation in his famous Sermon on the Mount. Matthew records Jesus saying, "You have heard that it was said, 'You shall love your neighbor and hate your enemy.' But I say to you, Love your enemies and pray for those who persecute you, so that you may be children of your Father in heaven" (Matt. 5:43–45). Referencing this Christian understanding of love, King describes the concept of *agapē*:

> *Agape* is understanding, creative, redemptive, good will toward all men. It is an overflowing love which seeks nothing in return. Theologians would say that it is the love of God operating in the human heart. So that when one rises to love on this level, he loves men not because he likes them, not because their ways appeal to him, but he loves every man because God loves him. And he rises to the point of loving the person who does an evil deed while hating the deed that the person does. I think this is what Jesus meant when he said "love your enemies."[37]

35. J. Deotis Roberts, *Liberation and Reconciliation: A Black Theology*, 2nd ed. (Louisville: Westminster John Knox, 2005), 62–63.

36. See Jason Horowitz, Nick Corasaniti, and Ashley Southall, "Nine Killed in Shooting at Black Church in Charleston," *New York Times*, June 17, 2015, https://www.nytimes.com/2015/06/18/us/church-attacked-in-charleston-south-carolina.html.

37. Martin Luther King Jr., "Love, Law, and Civil Disobedience" (address before the Fellowship of the Concerned, November 16, 1961), in *Testament of Hope*, 46–47.

King's formulation of *agapē* love is what Paris describes when writing, "He [King] contended that there would be no permanent solution to the race problem until oppressed people developed the capacity to love their enemies."[38]

In addition to addressing love in the Sermon on the Mount, Jesus also addresses forgiveness. In the Lord's Prayer, Matthew records Jesus teaching his listeners how to pray by saying, "And forgive us our debts, as we also have forgiven our debtors" (Matt. 6:12). In describing the Christian mandate of "biblical forgiveness"—something that is similar to King's "love of enemies" but distinct enough to be a conceptual cousin rather than a sibling—Anthony Thompson, an ordained minister and surviving spouse of one of the nine victims killed in the Mother Emanuel AME Church massacre, writes, "Unlike society's forgiveness that is packed with myths, biblical forgiveness has no strings attached to it. It is forgiveness without condition, needing no apology, no compensation for the loss, no face-to-face meeting, and no response from the offender. It is simply a victim's unquestioning forgiveness given as a gift of grace to the offender. . . . With biblical forgiveness, victims choose to forgive another person because they, themselves, have been completely forgiven by God. Their own sinful debt has been paid in full with no conditions—an underserved grace gift from their heavenly Father."[39]

In further reflecting on God's forgiving grace, Thompson also powerfully shares, "I have forgiven Dylann Roof completely because God has forgiven me completely. To society, this type of no-strings-attached forgiveness seems illogical. But to Christ-believers who have experienced God's loving and complete forgiveness, biblical forgiveness makes perfect sense."[40]

Thompson completely illustrates the nature of forgiveness as an element of reconciliation; to receive forgiveness from God, one must be willing to extend forgiveness to other humans. Indeed, in the Sermon on the Mount, Jesus says, "For if you forgive others their

38. Paris, *Black Religious Leaders*, 113.
39. Anthony B. Thompson, with Denise George, *Called to Forgive: The Charleston Church Shooting, a Victim's Husband, and the Path to Healing and Peace* (Minneapolis: Bethany House, 2019), 142.
40. Thompson, *Called to Forgive*, 142.

trespasses, your heavenly Father will also forgive you; but if you do not forgive others, neither will your Father forgive your trespasses" (Matt. 6:14–15).

Conclusion

Although forgiveness is never easy, genuine reconciliation—wherein the oppressed can be reconciled with the oppressor—necessities embracing a Christocentric ethic that is rooted in Jesus's Sermon on the Mount. For King, the salient and motivating takeaway was (*agapē*) love combined with a Gandhi-influenced nonviolent resistance. This Black church exemplar embraced civil disobedience, along with a suffering servant theology, to love oppressors while simultaneously hating their acts of oppression.

More recently, after the massacre at Mother Emanuel AME Church, a Black surviving spouse and clergyperson demonstrated biblical forgiveness in recognizing that, because *all* have sinned and fallen short of the glory of God, if humans want to receive forgiveness from God, they must be able to extend forgiveness to one another. To create balanced social relationships, people must see genuine forgiveness as an essential element of the church's work toward civil reconciliation.

PART 2

RECONCILIATION
WITH "THE OTHER"

FOUR

THE RESPONSE TO CIVIL RECONCILIATION

White Evangelicalism and the Southern Strategy
Give Rise to "Make America Great Again"

The Southern Strategy Meets "Make America Great Again"

In the wake of the successes of the Civil Rights Movement, the Black church's work toward civil reconciliation caused a white backlash—an effect that CNN political commentator Van Jones would later term a "whitelash."[1] As he campaigned for the presidency in 1968, Richard Nixon sought to gain political support among white voters in the South, who had traditionally been Democrats, by appealing to their distaste for the Black empowerment brought on by the passage of the Voting Rights Act of 1965.[2] This tactic, which became known as the southern strategy, appealed to the same sentiment that caused white flight from the cities to the suburbs in the South (and elsewhere in the country). With a white exodus from cities, Nixon and the

1. Van Jones coined this term on air during CNN's election-night coverage of the 2016 presidential election, once it became clear that Donald J. Trump would become the forty-fifth president of the United States.

2. Jemar Tisby describes this backlash in terms of a partisan reaction to the Black church's progressive politics. He describes how Nixon pointed to the Civil Rights Movement's nonviolent direct action as a "tarmac to tyranny and disregard for the law." *The Color of Compromise: The Truth about the American Church's Complicity in Racism* (Grand Rapids: Zondervan, 2019), 157.

Republican Party realized that votes from the suburbs were beginning to outnumber votes from both rural and urban areas. The strategy, therefore, was a direct appeal not to rural and working-class whites (who supported either Strom Thurman or George Wallace) but to middle-class suburbanites.[3] Nixon's successful campaign embraced the politics of white flight and sought to make an implicit cultural connection between the segregationist policies of the Old South and the Republican Party of the New South.

While embracing the biblical ethic that reconciliation is a ministry that Jesus left to the church (2 Cor. 5:17–19), the previous chapter explored civil reconciliation as putting faith into action in the public square. With forgiveness as a requisite, the church's work of civil reconciliation during the Civil Rights Movement involved both clergy and laity literally sacrificing themselves while also demanding governmental redress through policies and laws that sought to ensure full access to civic participation for *all people* in all aspects of American life. Among the most impactful and controversial of the measures achieved through their activism were the Voting Rights Act of 1965 and the policy of affirmative action.

The old cliché is true: "Every action has a reaction." The Civil Rights Movement's clergy-led work in civil reconciliation caused a white, working-class reaction that was also related to the church. Christian evangelicalism, popularized by Billy Graham, was co-opted by the partisan politics of Nixon's southern strategy as part of a response to minority advancement. The Republican Party's southern strategy was geared toward a demographic that increasingly included evangelicals in an attempt to mobilize conservative white Americans who held a post–Civil Rights Movement resentment toward Black communities.[4] This Republican Party exploitation of an anti–civil reconciliation sentiment in the late 1960s and early 1970s began a partisan political alignment that President Ronald Reagan solidified in the 1980s. These political and conservative evangelical factions courted and wed within the church. Their relationship was nurtured by the politics of Nixon and Reagan, and it ultimately gave birth to

3. Kevin M. Kruse, *White Flight: Atlanta and the Making of Modern Conservatism* (Princeton: Princeton University Press, 2005), 253.
4. Tisby, *Color of Compromise*, 157–58.

the "Religious Right" and the counternarrative popularly known as "Make America Great Again" (MAGA). It was this political and religious alliance that was responsible for the election of Donald Trump.

"Make America Great Again," Trump's 2016 campaign slogan, was aimed squarely at the bloc of voters who viewed the last half century's post–Civil Rights Movement changes as negative. In *The Great Alignment*, Alan Abramowitz notes that Trump promised to turn back the clock to a time when members of the white working class enjoyed greater influence and respect.[5] Moreover, although racial divisions in the United States are anything but new, Trump's incendiary campaign rhetoric capitalized on the racial enmity that was simmering during the Obama presidency.[6]

In *Stand Your Ground*, Kelly Brown Douglas writes of predictable pendulum swings after periods of racial progress that are consistent with a philosophy of Anglo-Saxon exceptionalism, as some factions have historically declared war against Black bodies invading their "space."[7] In chronologically tracing this pattern, from black codes after emancipation to the 2012 murder of Trayvon Martin after Obama's historic election, she writes,

> It is no accident that stand-your-ground culture has been most aggressively if not fatally executed after every period in which certain "rights" are extended to black people, ostensibly bringing them closer to enjoying the "inalienable rights of life, liberty, and the pursuit of happiness." This pattern of "white backlash" began with the

5. Alan I. Abramowitz, *The Great Alignment: Race, Party Transformation, and the Rise of Donald Trump* (New Haven: Yale University Press, 2018), 13.

6. In the years leading up to the 2016 presidential election, Donald Trump advanced the "birther movement," a verbal assault on Barack Obama's legitimacy as president of the United States supported by allegations that Obama's birth certificate was inauthentic, claiming Obama was actually born in Africa, not in the state of Hawaii. Moreover, while igniting xenophobic passions and appealing to the deepest forms of prejudice in the immigration debate, Trump also called Mexicans rapists and murderers, alleged immigration was in a state of crisis at the US/Mexico border, and said he would build a wall to keep Mexicans out of the United States and that Mexico would pay for it. See Kevin M. Kruse and Julian E. Zelizer, *Fault Lines: A History of the United States Since 1974* (New York: Norton, 2019), 333–34.

7. Kelly Brown Douglas, *Stand Your Ground: Black Bodies and the Justice of God* (Maryknoll, NY: Orbis Books, 2015).

emancipation. After emancipation, Black Codes, Jim Crow laws, and the heinous "punishment" of lynching was enforced. The "law and order" mandates of the post–civil rights era continued this pattern. White backlash surely is reflected in the virulent stand-your-ground reality that has followed the election of the first black president.[8]

Inasmuch as the culture Douglas references was energized by the Obama presidency, the predictable whitelash was realized in the MAGA narrative.[9]

Just as the Civil Rights Movement's work in civil reconciliation was at the intersection of law and religion, as faith communities demanded governmental action, the same can be said of the MAGA forces that led to Trump's presidency. Although there is arguably very little evidence of Trump being "religious," he was nonetheless able to capture the lion's share of white evangelical voters in the 2016 election, with promises to appoint Supreme Court justices who would overturn *Roe v. Wade*. Indeed, according to data from a national exit poll, white born-again or evangelical voters favored Trump over Hillary Clinton 80 percent to 16 percent.[10]

While pandering to what has become a politically predictable voting bloc during an October 2016 presidential debate, Trump unequivocally touted his pro-life stance in predicting *Roe v. Wade*'s demise. When debate moderator Chris Wallace pressed Trump on whether he wanted the ruling overturned, Trump was clear that it would happen "automatically" because he would get to appoint several justices to the Supreme Court.[11]

8. Douglas, *Stand Your Ground*, 117.

9. See, e.g., Peter Baker and Michael D. Shear, "El Paso Shooting Suspect's Manifesto Echoes Trump's Language," *New York Times*, August 4, 2019, https://www.nytimes.com/2019/08/04/us/politics/trump-mass-shootings.html; and Mehdi Hasan, "After El Paso, We Can No Longer Ignore Trump's Role in Inspiring Mass Shootings," *Intercept*, August 4, 2019, https://theintercept.com/2019/08/04/el-paso-dayton-mass-shootings-donald-trump. See also Caitlyn Oprysko, "Trump Rhetoric Freshly Condemned after Mass Shootings," POLITICO, August 4, 2019, https://www.politico.com/story/2019/08/04/beto-orourke-trump-el-paso-white-nationalist-1445700.

10. Abramowitz, *Great Alignment*, 11–12.

11. Dan Mangan, "Trump: I'll Appoint Supreme Court Justices to Overturn Roe v. Wade Abortion Case," CNBC, October 19, 2016, https://www.cnbc.com/2016/10/19/trump-ill-appoint-supreme-court-justices-to-overturn-roe-v-wade-abortion-case.html.

Although opposition to *Roe v. Wade* is now used to court evangelical voters, the great irony is that in the years immediately following the ruling, action against it did not pick up much steam. Instead, conservative voters coalesced around the issue of racial integration in schools after the IRS denied Bob Jones University's tax-exempt status because of its discriminatory policies.[12]

After the Supreme Court's 2013 decision in *Shelby County v. Holder* invalidated a key provision of the Voting Rights Act (the Civil Rights Movement's most empirical measure of success), several state legislatures enacted laws that had a restrictive effect on voting. According to the Brennan Center for Justice, for example, within twenty-four hours of the *Shelby County* ruling, Texas announced its plan to implement a strict photo ID law. Mississippi and Alabama announced they would do the same with respect to similar laws that had been barred because of the Voting Rights Act's federal preclearance protections.[13] In other words, with the elimination of accountability measures in certain jurisdictions with a proven history of voter discrimination, those same jurisdictions moved to enact restrictive voting laws with the only remedy being the slow process of litigation.

Most notably, North Carolina also attempted to impose a strict photo ID law as part of omnibus legislation that was later declared unconstitutional in targeting African American voters "with almost surgical precision."[14] While the North Carolina General Assembly used racial data to allow forms of identifications often held by whites but not allow forms of identification often held by Blacks, similar "discriminatory as applied" restrictive voting laws garnered popular media attention in 2021, in states like Georgia and Texas, after Trump's demonstrably false allegations that the November 2020 election was stolen. Voters used to choose their representatives. With

12. Tisby, *Color of Compromise*, 161.

13. See "The Effects of Shelby County v. Holder," Brennan Center for Justice, August 6, 2018, https://www.brennancenter.org/our-work/policy-solutions/effects-shelby-county-v-holder.

14. North Carolina State Conference of the NAACP v. McCrory, 831 F.3d 204, 214 (4th Cir. 2016); see also James L. Leloudis and Robert R. Korstad, *Fragile Democracy: The Struggle over Race and Voting Rights in North Carolina* (Chapel Hill: University of North Carolina Press, 2020), 116–19.

discriminatory photo ID laws in the wake of *Shelby County*, however, the representatives are the ones who are choosing their voters.

In the 2016 presidential election, the first held after the *Shelby County* ruling and the removal of the Voting Rights Act's protections, hurdles for minority voter participation worked to Trump's benefit. The minorities the Voting Rights Act sought to protect were the same minorities who were repeatedly targeted by Trump with race-based insults.

In this chapter, I connect theology, law, history, and political science in three sections. After this introduction, the first section gives an overview of the Voting Rights Act and affirmative action, two of the Civil Rights Movement's most successful but simultaneously controversial measures. Both progressive measures—examples of civil reconciliation—indirectly affected the church in that they caused a backlash in the form of a political fusion between white evangelical Christians and the Republican Party.

The second section shows the church's complicity in advancing a white nationalist agenda by exploring the political allegiance and partisan politics of white evangelical Christians and the Republican Party that resulted from the indirect work of Billy Graham and the very intentional work of Nixon's southern strategy. Indeed, the Make America Great Again narrative follows an established playbook for invoking the political support of evangelical Christians to undermine civil reconciliation's progress.

The third section addresses blatant attempts to frustrate civil reconciliation, highlighting some of the xenophobic divisions that led to Trump's 2016 election and his divisive style of governance. Indeed, Trump, more than any presidential candidate since George Wallace and Richard Nixon in 1968, reinforced some of the deepest social and cultural divisions within the American electorate.[15]

This chapter also concludes by laying a foundation for the solutions discussed in the following chapter. With signs of potential breaks between Trump-allied Republicans and evangelicals, it's time to reunite the church for the ministry of reconciliation to which she is called (2 Cor. 5:17–19). Stated otherwise, in response to the divisive cry to

15. Abramowitz, *Great Alignment*, 170.

"Make America Great Again," I present a unifying call to "Make the Church Great Again" by making it a space for diversity, inclusion, and cultural competency that can be an exemplar for society at large. The church must return to her apostolic origins of diversity and inclusivity if she is to fulfill her mission of both preaching salvation in the kingdom to come and remedying social inequities in the kingdom at hand.

The Voting Rights Act and Affirmative Action: Two of the Civil Rights Movement's Most Measurable Achievements in Civil Reconciliation

Although the leaders of the Civil Rights Movement presumably had many goals, their main goal was achieving full civic participation without racial discrimination. In moving toward freedom from oppression, the Voting Rights Act of 1965 has been the most quantifiable measure to date of civil reconciliation's success. And affirmative action has been arguably the most controversial means of pursuing civil reconciliation to emerge from America's freedom struggle.

The Voting Rights Act of 1965 and Its Role in Civil Reconciliation

Although the Fifteenth Amendment, ratified in 1870, prohibited states from denying a male citizen the right to vote based on "race, color, or previous condition of servitude," in the following decades various discriminatory practices were used to prevent Blacks, particularly those in the South, from exercising their right to vote. The Voting Rights Act of 1965, among other things, banned the use of literacy tests for voters, which had unfairly targeted Blacks.

In *The Dynamics of Racial Progress*, Antonine Joseph quantifies the Voting Rights Act's significance in ensuring that Blacks and other minorities were able to register and vote in elections, especially in the Deep South, arguing that, with the percentage of African American registered voters increasing from 22.5 percent to 65 percent, the Voting

Rights Act swamped the existing systems of disenfranchisement.[16] Similarly, in *Protest at Selma*, David Garrow quantifies the Voting Rights Act's significance in the weeks immediately following August 6, 1965 (the date President Lyndon Johnson signed it into law). He notes that by the end of August, there was a Black voter registration increase of more than sixty thousand in just the states of Alabama, Georgia, Louisiana, and Mississippi.[17] This alone illustrates the legislation's significance in moving toward the goal of full citizen participation.

In *Yick Wo v. Hopkins* (1886), the Supreme Court described the right to vote as fundamental in that it is "preservative of all rights."[18] In actuality, however, it wasn't until after the enactment of the Voting Rights Act—almost a century after ratification of the Fifteenth Amendment—that this right promised during Reconstruction become a reality. In *South Carolina v. Katzenbach* (1966), one of the first cases addressing the statute's constitutionality, the US Supreme Court wrote, "The Voting Rights Act was designed by Congress to banish the blight of racial discrimination in voting, which has infected the electoral process in parts of our country for nearly a century."[19] Insofar as the legislation was successful in achieving its intended purpose, the clergy-led movement that enabled its passage underscores civil reconciliation's multidisciplinary importance—it resulted in changes in American's legal landscape because people were motivated by faith. Indeed, as a legal reform that resulted from faith-based actions, the Voting Rights Act led to unprecedented inclusion and political participation. With this level of success, however, there would inevitably be opposition. The opposition was ultimately successful, as evidenced by the Supreme Court's 2013 decision in *Shelby County v. Holder*.

Recent Interpretations of the Voting Rights Act

The Voting Rights Act was an embodiment of civil reconciliation in allowing a diversity of perspectives in the electoral process,

---

16. Antoine L. Joseph, *The Dynamics of Racial Progress: Economic Inequality and Race Relations Since Reconstruction* (Armonk, NY: M. E. Sharpe, 2005), 126.
17. David Garrow, *Protest at Selma: Martin Luther King, Jr., and the Voting Rights Act of 1965* (New Haven: Yale University Press, 1978), 182.
18. Yick Wo v. Hopkins, 118 U.S. 365, 370 (1886).
19. South Carolina v. Katzenbach, 383 U.S. 301, 308 (1966).

fostering full civic participation. After the 2006 reauthorization of the act, however, the Supreme Court addressed two significant challenges to the statute's constitutionality in *Northwest Austin Municipal Utility District No. One v. Holder* (2009) and *Shelby County v. Holder* (2013). *Northwest Austin* laid the groundwork to undermine the legislation, and *Shelby County* struck a critical blow. Consequently, serious questions now exist as to whether the law even remains viable.

In *Northwest Austin*, the petitioner was a small utility district with an elected board. Because of its Texas location, it was considered a "covered jurisdiction" under the coverage formula of Section 4 of the Voting Rights Act, requiring federal preclearance before any changes to its election procedure could occur. Although the Court rejected the utility company's challenges to the constitutionality of Section 5— the Voting Rights Act's actual preclearance procedure—the Court significantly undermined the legislation by opining,

> The historic accomplishments of the Voting Rights Act are undeniable. When it was first passed, unconstitutional discrimination was rampant and the "registration of voting-age whites ran roughly 50 percentage points or more ahead" of black registration in many covered States. . . . Today, the registration gap between white and black voters is in single digits in the covered States; in some of those States, blacks now register and vote at higher rates than whites. . . . "Many of the first generation barriers to minority voter registration and voter turnout that were in place . . . have been eliminated."[20]

Consequently, although the *Northwest Austin* Court left the Voting Rights Act intact, it also forecasted the legislation's demise. Four years later, *Shelby County* picked up where *Northwest Austin* left off.

In *Shelby County*, the Court was again faced with a challenge to the constitutionality of Section 5. This time, however, the municipal petitioner—a county in Alabama—also challenged the coverage formula found in Section 4(b) of the Voting Rights Act, the formula that determined what geographic jurisdictions fell under the legislation's

20. Northwest Austin Municipal Utility District No. One v. Holder, 557 U.S. 193 (2009), 201.

protective purview. While leaving Section 5 intact, the Court's 5–4 majority granted the petitioner's request and invalided Section 4(b). The Court decided that although the Voting Rights Act had worked in the past, it had essentially run its course in that Section 4(b)'s coverage formula was antiquated and unconstitutional. It wrote, "Coverage today is based on decades-old data and eradicated practices. The formula captures States by reference to literacy tests and low voter registration and turnout in the 1960s and 1970s. But such tests have been banned nationwide for over 40 years."[21]

Although the Court did not invalidate Section 5, until Congress prescribes a new coverage formula to replace Section 4(b), no place is subject to Section 5's preclearance requirements. Therefore, the Voting Rights Act—empirically the most successful form of civil reconciliation—no longer has any teeth. *Shelby County* reduced it to watchdog legislation, allowing it to bark but eliminating its bite.

Affirmative Action and Its Role in Civil Reconciliation

No topic in constitutional law is more controversial than affirmative action. Because I regard affirmative action as a form of civil reconciliation, I see it as an imperfect governmental attempt to create the same type of diversity exemplified in the biblically based practice of social reconciliation—creating diversity and inclusion by putting people in relationship with the proverbial "Other." Conceptually, therefore, affirmative action is no different from when Peter, a Jew, was put in relationship with Cornelius, a gentile, as he was made to realize that God does not distinguish between persons (Acts 10:34). Indeed, with respect to the significance of reconciliation in Acts 10, John Perkins writes, "The apostle Peter struggled with the vision of reconciliation. He was steeped in Jewish culture, which had taught him to see non-Jews as unclean. But God opened his eyes to a new truth."[22] The policy of affirmative action was adopted to open the eyes of both Blacks and whites to "new truths" by breaking down social barriers and building commonality across racial lines.

21. Shelby County v. Holder, 570 U.S. 529, 551 (2013).
22. John Perkins, *One Blood: Parting Words to the Church on Race and Love* (Chicago: Moody, 2018), 33.

In *The Pursuit of Fairness*, the first historical analysis of affirmative action, Terry Anderson chronologically traces the policy from its genesis in the Great Depression and World War II through the Supreme Court's 2003 cases *Gratz v. Bollinger* and *Grutter v. Bollinger*. Expounding on the policy's controversial nature, Anderson writes, "It has been a public policy for four decades . . . and it always raises emotions, contentious debate, and all too often charges of racism. Both sides claim moral superiority. Supporters declare themselves the champions of racial justice, protectors of Martin Luther King's Dream, while opponents see themselves as the defenders of merit, of colorblind equal protection enshrined in the U.S. Constitution. One thing is clear: the arguments of both sides have merit and are legitimate, and that in itself makes affirmative action an American dilemma."[23] Reconciliation is difficult in most contexts. Its difficulty is definitely not surprising in the context of affirmative action.

To explain this complex policy, using the context of higher education,[24] I will explore three Supreme Court rulings: (1) *Regents of the University of California v. Bakke* (1978), the Court's seminal affirmative action case; (2) *Grutter v. Bollinger* (2003), a decision wherein Justice Sandra Day O'Connor expressly wrote, "We expect that 25 years from now, the use of racial preferences will no longer be necessary";[25] and (3) *Fisher v. University of Texas at Austin* (2013), the Court's most recent 5–4 decision regarding affirmative action's constitutionality in pursuing the laudable goal of diversity in higher education.

23. Terry H. Anderson, *The Pursuit of Fairness: A History of Affirmative Action* (New York: Oxford University Press, 2004), x.

24. I deliberately chose to contextualize affirmative action in higher education, as opposed to in employment or the construction industry, because colleges and professional schools play a preparatory role that is like that of the church. They place a subset of society in a place of social exposure that should broaden their capacity to understand others who come from different backgrounds. As is the case with professions such as law and medicine, the academic institution prepares students to interact with diverse populations by teaching them a service that has social value. The same can be said for the church. It too should prepare people to interact with diverse populations while also offering multiple things (e.g., evangelism, hope, mission work, etc.) that have social value.

25. Grutter v. Bollinger, 539 U.S. 306 (2003), 343.

Regents of the University of California v. Bakke (1978)

The University of California at Davis Medical School attempted to increase its incoming class diversity with two admissions programs for an entering class of one hundred students. There was a general admissions program and a separate special admissions program. If a minority applicant was found to be disadvantaged, they were evaluated under the special program instead of the regular one. Over the course of four years, forty-four minority students were admitted to Davis under the regular program, and sixty-three were admitted under the special program. No disadvantaged white applicants were admitted, although several applied. The litigation resulted from a constitutional challenge brought by Allen Bakke, a white male who unsuccessfully applied to Davis under the general admissions program in 1973 and 1974. He challenged the policy that reserved sixteen of the one hundred entering student slots for minority students, seeing it as violating his constitutional rights.

In expounding on the importance of diversity, especially in the context of an environment in which people are being formed and prepared to address social challenges in a very diverse society, the Court opined,

> Physicians serve a very heterogeneous population. An otherwise qualified medical student with a particular background—whether it be ethnic, geographic, culturally advantaged or disadvantaged—may bring to a professional school of medicine experiences, outlooks, and ideas that enrich the training of its student body and better equip its graduates to render with understanding their vital service to humanity.
>
> Ethnic diversity, however, is only one element in a range of factors a university properly may consider in attaining the goal of a heterogeneous student body.[26]

The Court clearly saw the importance of diversity in a laboratory-type social setting in which ideals and values are formed. Moreover, in addition to ethnic diversity, the Court's opinion opened the door for deliberate measures to pursue other kinds of diversity.

26. Regents of the University of California v. Bakke, 438 U.S. 265 (1978), 314.

Although in the *Bakke* decision the Court denied that race was the only important factor to consider in pursuing diversity, it affirmed that promoting racial diversity is indeed in the government's interest. Specifically, the Court wrote, "The State has a substantial interest that legitimately may be served by a properly devised admissions program involving the competitive consideration of race and ethnic origin."[27] Accordingly, the Supreme Court validated the importance of diversity in higher education in its first encounter with affirmative action in 1978.

Grutter v. Bollinger (2003)

In *Grutter v. Bollinger*, the Court evaluated the constitutionality of a University of Michigan Law School admissions policy that sought to achieve student body diversity in compliance with *Bakke*. The Michigan Law School received more than 3,500 applications for an entering class of approximately 350 students. In recognizing the value of diversity, the law school sought a mix of students with varying backgrounds and experiences. The Court noted that the hallmark of the admissions policy "is its focus on academic ability coupled with the flexible assessment of applicants' talents, experiences, and potential 'to contribute to the learning of those around them.'"[28] The petitioner was a white Michigan resident who was denied admission to the law school. She subsequently filed suit, alleging the admissions policy discriminated against her based on race, in violation of the Fourteenth Amendment's Equal Protection Clause.

In relying on *Bakke*, and again emphasizing the importance of diversity on college campuses, the Court reasoned,

> We have long recognized that, given the important purpose of public education and the expansive freedoms of speech and thought associated with the university environment, universities occupy a special niche in our constitutional tradition. . . . In announcing the principle of student body diversity as a compelling state interest, Justice Powell invoked our cases recognizing a constitutional dimension, grounded in the First Amendment of educational autonomy: "The

27. *Bakke*, 438 U.S. 265, at 320.
28. *Grutter*, 539 U.S. 306, at 315.

freedom of a university to make its own judgments as to education includes the selection of its student body." . . . From this premise, Justice Powell reasoned that by claiming "the right to select those students who will contribute the most to the 'robust exchange of ideas,'" a university "seek[s] to achieve a goal that is of paramount importance in the fulfillment of its mission."[29]

After closely evaluating the admissions policy's racial considerations and concluding that the law school properly considered all "pertinent elements of diversity," the Court found the policy constitutional while simultaneously suggesting that race-based considerations should sunset in the not-so-distant future.[30]

Fisher v. University of Texas at Austin (2013)

In *Fisher v. University of Texas at Austin* (2013), the Court again examined the issue of race consideration to achieve diversity—this time as a single element in a higher education admissions process. The Court recognized that although race was not itself assigned a numerical value for each applicant to the University of Texas, the institution had committed itself to increasing racial minority enrollment on campus, referring to its goal as a "critical mass."[31] Abagail Fisher, who was white, was one of 29,501 applicants for the 2008 entering class; 12,843 applicants were offered admission, with 6,715 accepting and enrolling. Fisher's application was denied, and she subsequently filed suit.

After the Supreme Court's rulings in *Grutter v. Bollinger* (2003) and *Gratz v. Bollinger* (2003),[32] the University of Texas began expressly considering race in its admissions process. The Court relied on *Grutter* to emphasize the importance of diversity in higher education and distinguished between affirmative action and any policy aimed at redressing past discrimination. The Court wrote, "The attainment of

29. *Grutter*, 539 U.S. 306, at 329.
30. *Grutter*, 539 U.S. 306, at 341–43.
31. Fisher v. University of Texas at Austin, 133 S. Ct. 2411, 2415 (2013).
32. In contrast to *Grutter*, the *Gratz v. Bollinger* Court invalidated the University of Michigan's undergraduate admissions policy, which automatically awarded points to applicants from certain racial minorities. See Gratz v. Bollinger, 539 U.S. 244 (2003).

a diverse student body . . . serves values beyond race alone, including enhanced classroom dialogue and the lessening of racial isolation and stereotypes. The academic mission of a university is 'a special concern of the First Amendment.' . . . Part of 'the business of a university is to provide that atmosphere which is most conducive to speculation, experiment, and creation' and this in turn leads to the question of who may be admitted to study."[33]

In again validating affirmative action, the Court expressly identified the value of diversity in an educational environment. The same should apply to the church, another social institution in which people interact with "Others" and learn from their interactions that God shows no partiality among people (Acts 10:34). In other words, just as the church engaged in reconciliation when the Jewish Peter moved past the limits of his ethnic experience and discovered commonality with the gentile Cornelius, affirmative action does the same thing. It allows various peoples to similarly establish community that is beyond their previous experiences.

Can the Church Be a Place of Diversity and Inclusion and an Exemplar for Society at Large?

Given the Supreme Court's current composition, the future of affirmative action seems bleak. Yet affirmative action's anticipated sunset creates a rare opportunity for the church to demonstrate inclusivity and cultural competency and, in doing so, to be an exemplar of diversity and inclusion for society at large. In *Disunity in Christ*, Christena Cleveland writes, "The voices in the world have become increasingly diverse and interconnected; churches should be ready to welcome and engage individuals who represent all aspects of this diversity."[34] Such an inclusive embrace is indeed the ministry of reconciliation that Jesus left to the church (2 Cor. 5:16–19).

Because of the way humans learn from one another, diversity and inclusion are particularly valuable. Humans grow by being in community with "the Other." As Cleveland writes, "Research shows

33. *Fisher*, 133 S. Ct., at 2418.
34. Christena Cleveland, *Disunity in Christ: Uncovering the Hidden Forces That Keep Us Apart* (Downers Grove, IL: InterVarsity, 2013), 42.

that sharing an experience with another person—sometimes called 'I-sharing'—causes people to feel a profound sense of connection with others, even others who are otherwise dissimilar. Even brief, seemingly inconsequential experiences can help you connect with others."[35] Moreover, as relevant studies show, "diverse groups, when formulated effectively, and when people have taken the time to learn to understand one another, communicate and work together effectively and produce better results with higher productivity and more creative problem solving."[36]

In addressing social diversity—groups with varied membership based on race, ethnicity, gender, and sexual orientation—Katherine Phillips writes, "*Diversity enhances creativity*. It encourages the search for novel information and perspectives, leading to better decision making and problem solving. Diversity can improve the bottom line of companies and lead to unfettered discoveries and breakthrough innovations. *Even simply being exposed to diversity can change the way you think*."[37] Moreover, in *The Wisdom of Crowds*, James Surowiecki argues that diverse groups of people make better decisions than individuals or homogeneous groups when it comes to (1) cognition problems—those that will have definite solutions; (2) coordination problems—those that require members of a group to coordinate their behavior with one another; and (3) cooperation problems—those involving the challenge of getting people to work together.[38] The literature supports the assertion that diversity is a good thing. It can be especially important for the church and its ministries that address societal problems such as food insecurity, poverty, and homelessness. This point will be developed further in the next chapter.

35. Cleveland, *Disunity in Christ*, 30.

36. Howard J. Ross, *ReInventing Diversity: Transforming Organizational Community to Strengthen People, Purpose, and Performance* (Lanham, MD: Rowman & Littlefield, 2011), 24 (citing Scott E. Page, *The Difference: How the Power of Diversity Creates Better Groups, Firms, Schools, and Societies* [Princeton: Princeton University Press, 2007]).

37. Katherine W. Phillips, "How Diversity Makes Us Smarter: Being Around People Who Are Different from Us Makes Us More Creative, More Diligent and Harder-Working," *Scientific American*, October 1, 2014, https://www.scientificameri can.com/article/how-diversity-makes-us-smarter (emphasis added).

38. See James Surowiecki, *The Wisdom of Crowds* (New York: Anchor Books, 2004), xvii–xviii.

Consider the opposite of diversity in an ecclesial context. In citing the applied research on groupthink of former Presbyterian minister Gerald Tritle, Cleveland writes, "According to Tritle, church leadership teams that make decisions in a homogeneous vacuum are more likely to make less-informed decisions while perceiving that their decision is superior to those of other groups. The perception that their decision is morally superior to those of other groups gives them license to adopt a narcissistic, defensive and inflexible stance that makes it nearly impossible for them to achieve unity with other cultural groups in the body of Christ."[39] If the church can create a space for productive dialogue, along with an atmosphere of diversity, inclusion, and cultural competency, then the church will be well on her way to fulfilling her ministry of reconciliation.[40]

Perkins also argues, based on select Scriptures, that *reconciliation in the church* looks like diversity in the church and that diversity in the church was always part of God's plan. He shares that from the beginning of Scripture to the end, the message of unity and diversity is woven into the whole fabric of God's creation. He writes, "Issues of justice, diversity, and reconciliation are not extra add-ons that the church can opt out of as a matter of personal preference. They are an essential part of the gospel."[41] Diversity is not only good for human interactions; it is also part of God's vision for the body of Christ.

Regretfully, however, the efforts toward civil reconciliation via the progressive politics of the Civil Rights Movement have created a pushback so that neither in the church nor in society at large have sides come closer together. Instead, they have been driven further apart by a fusion of white evangelical Christianity and partisan politics. Although some groups have clearly pushed against the fruits of civil reconciliation, there is still hope, given biblical and theological resources, that those groups might change. We now turn to the sociopolitical and religious circumstances that united white evangelicals and the Republican Party before asking whether this alliance is severable.

---

39. Cleveland, *Disunity in Christ*, 41.
40. In this, the church would also be embodying the wisdom reflected in the Supreme Court's decision in *Fisher v. University of Texas at Austin* (2013).
41. Perkins, *One Blood*, 19–20.

A Response to Success: The Southern Strategy Fusion of White Evangelicals and the Republican Party

The expression "evangelical Christian" is often used in political commentary without clarifying exactly who "evangelicals" are. And aside from occasional references to Reagan, commentators don't explain how the Republican Party formed an alliance with evangelical Christians. Here I attempt to identify evangelical voters, trace their relatively recent partisan allegiance, and raise the issue of whether that alliance can now be broken in order to move the church toward reconciliation.

In *The Color of Compromise*, Tisby reminds readers what white evangelicalism looked like only forty years ago, before the rise of the "Religious Right" (a politically conservative movement organized to respond to the liberal turn of the United States during the 1960s Civil Rights Movement): "Evangelicalism in America exploded during the 1970s and 1980s. The 'Jesus Movement' inspired a generation of college-age Christians to devote their lives to religion. President Jimmy Carter described himself as a 'born again' Christian and taught Bible study at his church. Newly formed evangelical megachurches, like Rick Warren's Saddleback Church in Orange County, started cropping up. Hal Lindsey's book *The Late Great Planet Earth*, based on a literal interpretation of biblical end-times prophecies, sold twenty-eight million copies. Evangelicals had so captured national attention that *Newsweek* magazine dubbed 1976 'The Year of the Evangelical.'"[42]

This means that as recently as the late 1970s, being an evangelical Christian had little if anything to do with politics, and it certainly wasn't associated with allegiance to a particular political party. That would obviously change.

So Who Are Evangelical Christians, Anyway?

In *The Evangelistic Love of God and Neighbor*, Scott Jones defines evangelism: "The Greek word *euangelos* from which 'evangelism' stems is normally translated as 'gospel' in English Bibles. The prefix

42. Tisby, *Color of Compromise*, 153–54.

eu means good and *angelos* means news, so the gospel is the good news of Jesus Christ."[43] Moreover, in *The Making of Evangelicalism*, Randall Balmer shares, "The term *evangelical*, at its root, refers to the gospel—the 'good news'—of the New Testament and, more specifically, to the four evangelists: Matthew, Mark, Luke and John."[44] Martin Luther's sixteenth-century "rediscovery of the gospel" gave the term and its usage a distinctly Protestant cast.[45] As Protestantism developed in the United States, American evangelicalism derived from an eighteenth-century confluence of Scots-Irish Presbyterianism, Continental Pietism, and the vestiges of New England Puritanism.[46]

Balmer identifies three tenets of American evangelicalism: "an embrace of the Holy Bible as inspired and God's revelation to humanity, a belief in the centrality of a conversion or 'born again' experience, and the impulse to evangelize or bring others to the faith."[47] In *Divided by Faith*, Michael Emerson and Christian Smith offer a similar description:

> In contrast to those who might cite human reason, personal experience, tradition, or individual preference as conclusive authorities for truth, evangelicals hold that the final, ultimate authority is the Bible. Stemming from this, evangelicals believe that Christ died for the salvation of all, and that anyone who accepts Christ as the one way to eternal life will be saved. This act of faith is often called being "born again" and is associated with a spirituality, and often more broadly, transformed life. And of course, true to their name, evangelicals believe in the importance of sharing their faith, or evangelizing.[48]

These characteristics are arguably consistent with modern-day connotations of evangelicalism and of what it means to be an "evangelical Christian."

43. Scott J. Jones, *The Evangelistic Love of God and Neighbor: A Theology of Witness and Discipleship* (Nashville: Abingdon, 2003), 23.

44. Randall Balmer, *The Making of Evangelicalism: From Revivalism to Politics and Beyond* (Waco: Baylor University Press, 2010), 2.

45. Balmer, *Making of Evangelicalism*, 2.

46. Balmer, *Making of Evangelicalism*, 2.

47. Balmer, *Making of Evangelicalism*, 2.

48. Michael O. Emerson and Christian Smith, *Divided by Faith: Evangelical Religion and the Problem of Race in America* (Oxford: Oxford University Press, 2000), 3.

Even with these common characteristics, however, evangelicalism is not static. It is diverse and malleable and has transformed with changing times.[49] Emerson and Smith share that evangelicalism has historically included such diverse groups as fundamentalists, Pentecostals, holiness people, charismatics, the sanctified tradition, neo-evangelicals, and various ethnic groups.[50] To understand how the diversity of evangelicalism changed and how evangelical Christians became so closely associated with Republican Party politics, it is important to note four distinct periods of evolution.

During the First and Second Great Awakenings, evangelicals dramatically revised their theology of salvation and began focusing on individual behaviors in a millennial kingdom (a kingdom that they thought of as being a present reality not only here on earth in general but in America in particular). This was followed by a late nineteenth-century period of dispensational premillennialism—a rapture theology of Jesus's imminent return, in anticipation of a thousand-year reign of peace. It was during this period that the evangelical focus turned inward as evangelicals became more estranged from the dominant culture.[51] In the 1970s, the evangelical subculture had a turning point, with its timid embrace of Jimmy Carter, a Southern Baptist Sunday school teacher, serving as a link to secular politics. As Balmer notes, however, by the late 1970s evangelicals had shifted away from their roots and embraced right-wing political conservatism.[52] This last evangelical shift can be traced to Nixon's southern strategy in the late '60s and early '70s and to Reagan's political charisma leading up to the 1980 presidential election. But

---

49. In noting the flexibility of evangelicalism, implying its ability to evolve, as it has, over time, Balmer writes, "One of the reasons evangelicalism is so pliable is that, unlike other religious traditions, it is not (for the most part) bound by ecclesiastical hierarchies, creedal formulas, or liturgical rubrics. For many evangelicals, even the word *tradition* has a negative valence; it suggests a kind of stultifying, calcified rigor that somehow, evangelicals believe, inhibits a true and dynamic embrace of the faith." *Making of Evangelicalism*, 3.

50. Balmer, *Making of Evangelicalism*, 3. Emerson and Smith share a caveat with respect to the diversity of evangelical Christians. They write, "Evangelicals come from all ethnic and racial backgrounds, but nearly 90 percent of Americans who call themselves evangelicals are white." *Divided by Faith*, 3.

51. Balmer, *Making of Evangelicalism*, 4–5.

52. Balmer, *Making of Evangelicalism*, 5–6.

how did these factors work to forge an alliance between what was once a diverse religious movement and a political movement that opposed further advancing the reconciliation work represented by the Civil Rights Movement?

How Evangelical Christianity Became Aligned with the Political Right

In response to the 1960s' most measurable achievements in civil reconciliation, the Voting Rights Act and the government's attempts at diversity and inclusion by means of affirmative action, an unlikely alliance began to develop. The Republican Party's southern strategy capitalized on an anti-progress sentiment, associated with the Black church's political activism in the Civil Rights Movement, by creating a fusion between disgruntled whites and evangelical Christians. Over the course of four decades, this unlikely alliance became a bedrock constituency of the Republican Party.

Although born of social resentment, the evangelical Christian–Republican Party alliance was solidified by "morality" in opposition to abortion. In other words, although Nixon's "law and order" political rhetoric in the late 1960s helped create the alliance, it was solidified by Reagan's deliberate efforts to make evangelicals a solid Republican Party voting bloc by opposing *Roe v. Wade*. That alliance led Reagan to victory in 1980 over the incumbent president, Jimmy Carter. That same alliance has become even more solidified in the almost forty years since, and it led Trump to victory over Hillary Clinton in 2016.

To understand how evangelicalism became so closely associated with Republican Party politics, it is important to conceptualize three post–World War II sociopolitical shifts that were closely aligned with "revivalist nationalism," a sociopolitical theology that viewed America as God's chosen land that embraced a philosophy of treating her as such. Daniel Hummel chronicles these moves after detailing Billy Graham's famous 1949 Los Angeles crusade as a foundation. He writes about how revivalist nationalism maintained a central place in evangelical Christian nationalism and how by the 1960s and 1970s, Bill Bright, the founder of Campus Crusade for Christ, had transformed Graham's message to serve a political alliance with revival

campaigns that were specifically linked to the party politics of elect-
ing "men and women of God" in every position of influence. By
the 1980 presidential campaign, Jerry Falwell had taken Graham's
original soul-saving revivalist nationalism and aligned it with the
politics of his Moral Majority.[53] The last of the three shifts resulted
in the white evangelical community embracing Ronald Reagan and
laying the foundation for a fusion of partisan politics and evangelical Christianity.

In *Hijacked*, Mike Slaughter and Chuck Gutenson document the
phenomenon of evangelicals' allegiance to Republican candidates
that originated after passage of the Voting Rights Act. They write,
"White evangelical Protestant churches have undergone a dramatic
transformation since the mid-1960s. Just before passage of the 1965
Voting Rights Act, white evangelical Protestants self-identified as
68% Democratic, 25% Republican, and 7% Independent—making
up a significant part of what was referred to at the time as 'the solid
Democratic South.'"[54] In further documenting this shift, while implicitly referencing Nixon and expressly identifying Reagan as catalysts
for change, they write about Reagan's 1980 presidential campaign as
a watershed moment that marked the beginning of white evangelical Protestants becoming a bedrock constituency of the Republican
Party.[55]

While Carter made evangelicalism fashionable as a 1976 presidential candidate, drawing media attention to a previously overlooked
voting bloc, Reagan worked to gain evangelical support in the 1980
election as Carter's political prospects plummeted due to his unpopu-
lar handling of matters such as the Iran hostage crisis. In *One Nation
under God*, Kevin Kruse describes how Reagan built an evangelical
alliance with the Republican Party:

> In the lead-up to the 1980 election, a Gallop poll revealed an electorate
> in the midst of a religious revival. More than 80 percent of Americans

53. Daniel Hummel, "Revivalist Nationalism since World War II: From 'Wake Up,
America!' to 'Make America Great Again,'" *Religions* 7, no. 11 (November 1, 2016):
2–3, https://www.mdpi.com/2077–1444/7/11/128.

54. Mike Slaughter and Charles E. Gutenson, *Hijacked: Responding to the Partisan Church Divide* (Nashville: Abingdon, 2012), 4.

55. Slaughter and Gutenson, *Hijacked*, 4.

accepted the divinity of Jesus Christ, almost half professed confidence in the inerrancy of the Holy Bible, and most surprisingly, nearly a third identified themselves as having a "born-again" experience of their own. . . .

Reagan resolved to win the votes of this newly discovered "religious right" at all costs. . . . Reagan quickly made common cause with leaders on the religious right such as Jerry Falwell, head of the Moral Majority organization, and worked to convert rank-and-file religious conservatives to his campaign.[56]

Through its examination of the devaluation of Black life, the Black Lives Matter movement has helped us see how America's undergirding Anglo-Saxon exceptionalism ran through both Nixon's "law and order" rhetoric and Reagan's "War on Drugs." Both were means of covertly leveraging anti-Black sentiment for the purpose of partisan politics. With them, Republicans reimaged the Civil Rights Movement's progress as lawlessness, which they then used as a justification for adopting racist policies without ever needing to talk directly about race.[57]

In *Fault Lines*, Kevin Kruse and Julian Zelizer provide further context that clarifies Reagan's political union with evangelical voters. They note that although there was no formal "Christian caucus" at the 1980 GOP convention, it was evident that Reagan had been warmly embraced by the forces of religious conservatism in that there was substantial overlap between his campaign and the political wishes of evangelical Christians.[58] This 1980s fusion of piety and political partisanship was turning evangelical Christianity into a predictable, bedrock constituency of the Republican Party.[59] Continually mobilized by an almost united interest in overturning *Roe v. Wade*, this constituency was again fired up and leveraged by the MAGA political extremism of the 2016 presidential campaign.[60]

56. Kevin M. Kruse, *One Nation under God: How Corporate America Invented Christian America* (New York: Basic Books, 2015), 277–78.

57. Douglas, *Stand Your Ground*, 125–26.

58. Kruse and Zelizer, *Fault Lines*, 104.

59. Abramowitz, *Great Alignment*, 10–11.

60. "Exit polls show white evangelical voters voted in high numbers for Donald Trump, 80 to 16 percent." Sarah Pulliam Bailey, "White Evangelicals Voted

Can Anything Separate Evangelicals from Blind Political Allegiance?

For evangelical Christians to move toward reconciliation with the mainline church and separate themselves from their forty-year allegiance with partisan politics, it would take not only a monumental event but also the laying bare of major contradictions. Trump's personal contradictions, much more than any of his off-color politics, have seemingly started a break. Consider a contrast between the two.

Trump's Abrasive Politics and Divisive Policies

Kruse and Zelizer describe "the Trump Phenomenon" by writing about events in the lead-up to the 2016 presidential election, including Trump's angry rhetoric on subjects such as undocumented Mexican immigrants and "thugs" in Baltimore. Documenting some of the MAGA violence that almost forecast the January 6, 2021, insurrection at the US Capitol, they write,

> At an October 2015 rally in Richmond, Virginia, Trump supporters ripped signs from Latino immigration activists; one spit in a protester's face. In November, an African American protester at a Birmingham rally was punched, kicked, and choked. At a December event in Las Vegas, when a black protester was being forcibly removed by security, Trump supporters screamed "light the motherf——er on fire!" Rather than try to reduce the violence, Trump rationalized it. After the Birmingham incident, for instance, he defended the crowd's assault on the protester, saying "maybe he *should* have been roughed up, because it was absolutely disgusting what he was doing."[61]

Trump's abrasive and dehumanizing politics were seemingly immaterial for many of his political supporters.

In addition to Trump's politics, his *policies* also proved to be xenophobic, exacerbating divisions in America—the very antithesis

---

Overwhelmingly for Donald Trump, Exit Poll Shows," *Washington Post*, November 9, 2016, https://www.washingtonpost.com/news/acts-of-faith/wp/2016/11/09/exit-polls -show-white-evangelicals-voted-overwhelmingly-for-donald-trump.

61. Kruse and Zelizer, *Fault Lines*, 335 (emphasis in original; expletive altered).

of reconciliation. He campaigned on building a US/Mexico border wall after calling Mexicans criminals and rapists.[62] Early on in his presidency, Trump stoked emotions with his prejudicial and divisive rhetoric regarding immigration policy. The authors of *Identity Crisis* chronicle how, after his outspoken campaign promise to limit immigration, even prior to his six-month mark in office, Trump was already looking for a list of how many immigrants had received visas to enter the United States in 2017. Trump said that immigrants from Nigeria would never "go back to their huts," only to be followed by a discussion on protections for immigrants from Haiti, El Salvador, and Africa, wherein Trump asked, "Why are we having all these people from shithole countries come here?"[63] This anti-reconciliation narrative should be problematic for those who take the Bible seriously.

Trump's Personal Contradictions

Trump's personal character should likewise cause alarm for evangelicals. In the wake of his historic December 18, 2019, impeachment by the US House of Representatives, a scathing Trump spoke at a political rally in Battle Creek, Michigan. Recounting a conversation with Democratic US Representative Debbie Dingell of Michigan, the widow of and successor to former representative John Dingell, Trump suggested that perhaps the late congressman was "looking up" at them (i.e., from hell).[64] Trump's comments drew criticism,

62. Michelle Ye Hee Lee, "Donald Trump's False Comments Connecting Mexican Immigrants and Crime," *Washington Post*, July 8, 2015, https://www.washingtonpost.com/news/fact-checker/wp/2015/07/08/donald-trumps-false-comments-connecting-mexican-immigrants-and-crime.

63. John Sides, Michael Tesler, and Lynn Vavreck, *Identity Crisis: The 2016 Presidential Campaign and the Battle for the Meaning of America* (Princeton: Princeton University Press, 2018), 201–2.

64. Associated Press, "Trump Takes Swipe at House Lawmaker's Dead Husband, Implying He's in Hell during Michigan Rally. The White House Says the President Was 'Just Riffing,'" *Chicago Tribune*, December 19, 2019, https://www.chicagotribune.com/midwest/ct-donald-trump-john-debbie-dingell-20191219-46rveqe42ne wrkcnnm52dr6zai-story.html. See also Caroline Kelly and Allie Malloy, "Trump Implies That the Late Rep. John Dingell Is 'Looking Up' from Hell," CNN, December 19, 2019, https://www.cnn.com/2019/12/18/politics/trump-rally-john-dingell-hell/index.html.

even from Republicans.[65] In the political aftermath, some evangelicals questioned whether Trump's character would allow them to continue supporting him.

In writing to evangelical Christians in December 2019, Mark Galli, the editor in chief of *Christianity Today* (a magazine founded by Billy Graham), squarely called out Trump's immorality and called for him to be removed from office. Referring to the incident that led to Trump's 2019 impeachment by the House of Representatives, Galli detailed Trump's obvious abuse of political power to coerce a foreign government into discrediting his then expected 2020 rival, Joe Biden. He also wrote about Trump's immoral relationships with women. Attempting to address any remaining evangelical justification for supporting Trump despite personal misgivings, including the justification that it was worth supporting him because he could nominate conservative justices to the Supreme Court, Galli challenged evangelicals to "consider what an unbelieving world will say if you continue to brush off Mr. Trump's immoral words and behavior in the cause of political expediency."[66] This unequivocal call for evangelicals to withdraw their support from Trump may be the first major sign of the unraveling of the closely bound alliance between evangelicals and the Republican Party that has existed for more than forty years. Galli's editorial was appreciated by some evangelicals, but it sparked a rebuke from others, who rallied to Trump's defense—revealing divisions within a once solid Republican constituency.

When looking critically at whether the alliance of the Republican Party and white evangelicals is severable, two schools of thought emerge. One is that Republicans and white evangelicals might "need each other" given the changing demographics of the United States. Because white evangelical Protestants were a third of the Republican base, Trump needed them to get elected. Many actually attribute the early support Trump received from Jerry Falwell Jr., then president

65. Kadia Goba, "Republicans Said It Was 'Inappropriate' for Trump to Attack a Member of Congress and Her Late Husband," *Buzzfeed*, December 19, 2019, https://www.buzzfeednews.com/article/kadiagoba/republicans-inappropriate-trump-dingell-hell-comment.

66. Mark Galli, "Trump Should Be Removed from Office," *Christianity Today*, December 19, 2019, https://www.christianitytoday.com/ct/2019/december-web-only/trump-should-be-removed-from-office.html.

of Liberty University and an influential evangelical voice,[67] as a reason for Trump's 2016 victory. Because white evangelicals might see themselves as a shrinking minority, in both racial and religious terms, they might feel that they need to stick with the Republican Party in order to hold on to power and influence in society.

The other school of thought is that the unearthed division between Republicans and evangelicals will continue to grow in years to come due to the changing attitudes of younger evangelicals. Many younger evangelical Christians are more socially liberal on issues such as same-sex marriage, and they were troubled by the MAGA policies of separating migrant children from their families at the border and denying the existence of climate change. As the *New York Times* highlighted, "Evangelicals who are troubled by the president's conduct said they feared he had done long-term damage to their cause, and that the lack of pushback had only hurt them more, especially with young people."[68]

Evangelical Christianity, just like other religious factions within the church, is not monolithic. Trump's personal conduct and some of his policies have created divisions among evangelicals. These divisions present significant opportunities for progressive evangelicals to move toward social reconciliation with mainline Protestants and to partner with them in the work of civil reconciliation.

Conclusion

With the United States experiencing intense divisions, it seems that the backlash from progress toward civil reconciliation has fractured both society at large and the church. Although religious and social factions in the United States have been united by identity politics,

67. Falwell resigned from his position as president of Liberty University in August 2020 following public revelations of alleged sexual misconduct. See "Jerry Falwell Jr. Resigns from Liberty University. Again," *Religion News Service*, August 24, 2020, https://religionnews.com/2020/08/24/jerry-falwell-resigns-liberty-university-alleged-affair-trump-pool-attendant/.

68. Elizabeth Dias and Jeremy W. Peters, "Evangelical Leaders Close Ranks with Trump after Scathing Editorial," *New York Times*, December 20, 2019, https://www.nytimes.com/2019/12/20/us/politics/christianity-today-trump-evangelicals.html.

the depth of ethnic and political divisions has been intensified by the Make American Great Again political narrative and by the tragic killings of the many unarmed Blacks that gave rise to the Black Lives Matter movement. The question is now whether the first major sign of a break between evangelicals and the Republican Party will result in a return to the unity of diversity manifested in the early church.

If younger evangelicals are truly disturbed by the immorality of policies such as separating migrant children from their families, opposition to same-sex marriage, and denial of the existence of climate change, then one may question whether the Republican Party's partnership with white evangelicals will continue in the future, whether evangelicals will remain for Republicans a loyal, bedrock constituency. Although the church has never been monolithic, in light of such polarized factions, we must ask, Can the church embrace a theology of diversity, inclusion, and cultural competence in ways that would both be faithful to the gospel's call and serve as an exemplar for the secular world? I optimistically explore this possibility in the concluding chapter, "Where Do We Go from Here?"

FIVE

WHERE DO WE GO FROM HERE?

A Call for the Church to Return to Her Apostolic-Era Embrace of Diversity and Inclusion

In *Where Do We Go from Here* (his fourth and final book), Martin Luther King Jr. reflects on much of the progress made in America during the Civil Rights Movement while also looking at the obstacles the country still needed to overcome. In noting that social progress never moves in a straight line, King compares progress to a curvy road: sometimes you feel like you lose sight of the approaching goal, but you're still moving ahead and toward a destination.[1] That indeed has been the case as America moves toward reconciliation.

The rhetorical question "Where do we go from here?" requires introspective contemplation. "From here" suggests that there was progress or advancement, or some other kind of change, "back there." King completed *Where Do We Go from Here* in 1967, after the progress made by the Civil Rights Movement he helped lead, including the Civil Rights Act of 1964, the Elementary and Secondary Education Act of 1965, and the Voting Rights Act of 1965—all legislation aimed at making the United States a more diverse and

1. Martin Luther King Jr., *Where Do We Go from Here: Chaos or Community?* (1968; repr., Boston: Beacon, 2010), 12–13.

inclusive place for all people. Because King was assassinated in April 1968, he did not live to see the full fruits of his labor.

The Acts 2 and 10 narratives—exemplifying the church's work in social reconciliation—and the church's civil-rights-era work toward civil reconciliation reveal a shared realization "that all [people] are created equal, that they are endowed by their Creator with certain inalienable Rights, that among these are Life, Liberty and the pursuit of Happiness."[2] If all people are created equal in the sight of God— regardless of race or ethnicity, gender or sexual orientation, political affiliation or socioeconomic status—then the Acts 10 narrative must again be lived out in the church. "God shows no partiality, but in every nation anyone who fears him and does what is right is acceptable to him" (Acts 10:34–35).

As America continues to engage in conversations on race and social equity after the tragic murders of Breonna Taylor, Ahmaud Arbery, and George Floyd (among others) and the disparities revealed through the COVID-19 pandemic, including inequities that have affected vaccine distribution, in this chapter I return to King's question: "Where do we go from here?" In the name of reconciliation, I call on the church to return to her apostolic origins of diversity and inclusion in order to keep moving toward her destination, no matter how curvy the road might be.

The preceding chapters discussed three forms of reconciliation: (1) *salvific*—humans being reconciled to God through Jesus; (2) *social*—humans being reconciled to one another because of Jesus; and (3) *civil*—humans seeking governmental redress for social ills. In the last chapter, I detailed how the success of civil reconciliation led to opposition in the form of an alliance between white evangelical Christians and the Republican Party. This coalition originated with Richard Nixon's southern strategy and was solidified by Ronald Reagan's alliance with the Religious Right. Now, however, because of how the MAGA narrative has drawn on and inflamed a racial animus that undermines all of America's progress toward civil reconciliation, this alliance has led to a dan-

---

2. The Declaration of Independence, July 4, 1776, https://www.archives.gov /founding-docs/declaration-transcript.

gerous extremism. It helped fuel the hateful and ultimately deadly Unite the Right rally in Charlottesville, Virginia, in 2017. It helped mainstream the kind of racist nativism that inspired a gunman to specifically target Mexican nationals and Mexican Americans at a Walmart in El Paso, Texas, in 2019. And in a most unprecedented manner, MAGA extremism boiled over in an ultimately failed yet deadly insurrection at the US Capitol on January 6, 2021. Yet Donald Trump's divisive politics and character seem to have weakened the evangelical–Republican Party alliance. This is especially true for younger evangelicals and those focused more on individual rights than on communal morality.

In elaborating on research findings in the wake of the 2016 presidential election, Andrew Lewis writes, "Evangelical leaders who opposed Trump often cited his intolerance for others, while those who endorsed him claimed that he was the most capable of defending evangelicals' rights. Tolerance for others, and its importance, thus is a demarcation point dividing strong evangelical support for Trump and reluctant evangelical supporters or those who vowed never to support him (Never Trumpers)."[3] By therefore asking "Where do we go from here?" I am attempting to move the church toward reconciliation by challenging her more tolerant evangelicals to move toward a theology of equality, diversity, and inclusion that is rooted in the church's apostolic origins. In the words of John Perkins, "Issues of justice, diversity, and reconciliation are not extra add-ons that the church can opt out of as a matter of personal preference. They are an essential part of the gospel."[4]

To see how diversity and inclusion practices can help the church, consider Scott Page's advocacy for diversity in organizations. In *The Difference*, Page writes from the premise that diversity is fundamentally good for organizational breadth as he describes *identity diversity* (differences based on race and ethnicity) and *cognitive diversity*

---

3. Andrew R. Lewis, "Divided over Rights: Competing Evangelical Visions for Twenty-First Century America," in *The Evangelical Crackup? The Future of the Evangelical-Republican Coalition*, ed. Paul A. Djupe and Ryan L. Claassen (Philadelphia: Temple University Press, 2018), 81.

4. John M. Perkins, *One Blood: Parting Words to the Church on Race and Love* (Chicago: Moody, 2018), 19–20.

(differences based on background and training or life experiences) as being essential for problem solving.[5]

In advocating for both identity diversity and cognitive diversity, Page discusses *Grutter v. Bollinger* (2003), the University of Michigan Law School affirmative action case highlighted in chapter 4. Page disagrees with the late Associate Justice Antonin Scalia's dissenting opinion in *Grutter*, as Scalia suggests that identity diversity and cognitive diversity are at odds, that one can't have a "super-duper" law school that is simultaneously racially diverse. Page rebukes Scalia's logic: "Diversity and super-duperness can go hand in hand: a great law school may require a diversity of perspectives, interpretations, heuristics, and predictive models. A great law school benefits from including people with diverse preference. . . . So if we believe that differences in race, gender, ethnicity, physical ability, religion, sexual orientation, and so on correlate with cognitive diversity, then being super-duper *may* require some identity diversity. And, moreover, super-duperness may *always* require identity diversity, long after discrimination ends."[6] Page insists that identity diversity and cognitive diversity are also essential for organizations such as universities because they prepare people to serve society, and society is diverse.

The church has a similar social function. It too must prepare people to serve a diverse society. Therefore, it must be diverse itself. When we consider the respective backgrounds of the original disciples Jesus called to ministry (cognitive diversity) as well as the ethnic and geographic backgrounds of those who responded to Peter's call in beginning the church (identity diversity), we see that God intended the church to be diverse.

This chapter proceeds in three sections. After this introductory overview, the first section looks at God's intention for the church, through a diversity and inclusion lens, by exploring the scripturally based concept that the *ekklēsia* is a place of welcome for the proverbial "Other," especially those "from every nation, from all tribes and peoples and languages" (Rev. 7:9). To illustrate how God intends for

---

5. Scott E. Page, *The Difference: How the Power of Diversity Creates Better Groups, Firms, Schools, and Societies* (Princeton: Princeton University Press, 2007), 12–18.

6. Page, *Difference*, 17 (emphasis in original).

the church to be a place of welcome, I explore the diversity of the church militant and the church triumphant in Revelation.

The second section looks at some leading diversity and inclusion perspectives that point to diverse organizations being better for long-term problem solving and creating sustainable solutions. The diversity that is good for secular institutions can also be good for the church.

The third section looks at whether the current church is moving in the direction God would have her go by exploring church-based reconciliation. I look at evangelical factions and argue that, notwithstanding evangelicals' overwhelming support of political extremism in 2016 and 2020, white evangelical Christians are becoming *less separate* and *more tolerant* of "the Other" in their social views. Accordingly, even though a complete break of the evangelical Christian–Republican Party coalition is unlikely, evangelicals' recent advocacy for the rights of others strongly indicates that evangelical Christians are embracing what Perkins calls "biblical reconciliation": the removal of tension between parties and a return to loving relationships.[7]

In the New Testament, 1 John rebukes social enmity by clearly stating, "Those who say, 'I love God,' and hate their brothers and sisters, are liars; for those who do not love a brother or sister whom they have seen, cannot love God whom they have not seen. The commandment we have from him is this: those who love God must love their brothers and sisters also" (4:20–21). In expounding on this passage and addressing the core ethic of what I have termed social reconciliation, Will Willimon writes, "In loving we are surprised to have the Other move from being a stranger or enemy to the status of sister or brother. In attempting to love the Other, we find ourselves drawn closer to the God of love; we become as we profess. Love of neighbor validates that we are loving the true and living God rather than some godlet of our own concoction."[8]

The ability to engage in a ministry of welcome and give love to "the Other"—regardless of their race, ethnicity, social class, gender,

7. Perkins, *One Blood*, 17, 28.

8. William H. Willimon, *Fear of the Other: No Fear in Love* (Nashville: Abingdon, 2016), 11.

sexual orientation, or political partisanship—is at the heart of what the church's ministry of reconciliation is all about (2 Cor. 5:18–19). Accordingly, the third section concludes by looking at practical examples of how the church can move toward reconciliation and be an exemplar for society at large.

Finally, the conclusion refocuses attention on some of the biblically based concepts of social reconciliation, previously detailed in chapter 2, that may unite evangelicals and more mainline Christians in moving the church toward reconciliation. The conclusion also opens the door to the book's epilogue, where I explore how some of the 2020 and 2021 events influenced and are influencing the opinions of both Black and white evangelical voters.

What Did God Intend the Church to Look Like?

In asking the question, What did God intend the church to look like? we should begin with the recognition that the church is and has long been in a divided state. Many of the church's man-made[9] divisions are diametrically opposed to God's vision for the church. In *Disunity in Christ*, Christena Cleveland addresses these divisions, illustrating the fractured nature of the church in a jocular way as she retells Emo Phillip's popular joke (which *GQ* magazine named the forty-fourth funniest joke of all time):

> I was walking across a bridge one day and I saw a man standing on the edge, about to jump off. So I ran over and said, "Stop! Don't do it!"
> "Why shouldn't I?" he asked.
> "Well, there's so much to live for."
> "Like what?"
> "Well, are you religious?"
> He said yes.
> I said, "Me too! Are you Christian or Buddhist?"
> "Christian."
> "Me too! Are you Catholic or Protestant?"
> "Protestant."
> "Me too! Are you Episcopalian or Baptist?"

9. Most of the culprits here are, in fact, men.

"Baptist."

"Wow, me too! Are you Baptist Church of God or Baptist Church of the Lord?"

"Baptist Church of God!"

"Me too! Are you original Baptist Church of God or Reformed Baptist Church of God?"

"Reformed Baptist Church of God!"

"Me too! Are you Reformed Baptist Church of God, reformation 1879, or Reformed Baptist Church of God, reformation 1915?"

He said, "Reformed Baptist Church of God, reformation 1915!"

I said, "Die, heretic," and pushed him off.[10]

This indeed illustrates just how prone humans can be to focus on differences rather than celebrate diversity.

Here I explore diversity and reconciliation from a scriptural perspective by looking at the church militant and the church triumphant and urging the church to create what Howard Ross, in *Reinventing Diversity*, calls "organizational community": a place that welcomes diversity and inclusivity through a variety of factors, including collaboration.[11]

As a contrast to the underlying division at the heart of the joke above, the book of Revelation suggests that God intended for *all* people to be welcome in what would become the *ekklēsia*. John presents an impassioned critique of the oppressive political, religious, and socioeconomic realties of the Roman Empire as he writes from the penal colony of Patmos. Revelation unveils the vision of a world in the making—a vision of justice and peace embodied in a new heaven, a new earth, and a new Jerusalem—while delivering a rhetorically charged challenge for believers to withdraw from the empire and to live even now in the worship and service of the God who is making all things new.[12]

---

10. Christena Cleveland, *Disunity in Christ: Uncovering the Hidden Forces That Keep Us Apart* (Downers Grove, IL: InterVarsity, 2013), 32–33.

11. Howard J. Ross, *Reinventing Diversity: Transforming Organizational Community to Strengthen People, Purpose, and Performance* (Lanham, MD: Rowman & Littlefield, 2011), 191–203.

12. See David Rhoads, introduction to *From Every People and Nation: The Book of Revelation in Intercultural Perspective*, ed. David Rhoads (Minneapolis: Fortress, 2005), 1.

In theorizing that Revelation was written through a lens of cognitive dissonance, Harry Maier argues, "John composed Revelation to comfort Christians in Asia Minor who were being oppressed as a consequence of their refusal to acknowledge the divine claims of the emperor or to participate in his imperial cult. John thus urged them to hold fast and he held up for them the promise of divine reward."[13] Consequently, scholars traditionally date Revelation to the later part of Emperor Domitian's reign, between 92 and 96 CE, when Domitian promoted the Roman cult of emperor worship.[14]

Revelation 7 describes both the *church militant* (those called into political resistance against Rome's imperial domination; vv. 1–8) and the *church triumphant* (those who have transcended the great ordeal and have been rewarded for their labor; vv. 9–17). John invokes imagery reminiscent of the Hebrew Scriptures (Jer. 49:36; Zech. 6:5; Ezek. 9:4) and references the symbolic number of 144,000 people receiving the seal of God on their foreheads. In explaining this symbolism, Jean-Pierre Ruiz states, "The square of 12 multiplied by 1,000 has been interpreted variously as a reference to the faithful remnant of Israel; the church; the martyrs; the remnant of Christians who survive the eschatological turmoil; all of the redeemed."[15] Although this number may seem small by contemporary standards, to John's original audience it would have signified a vast number. Eugene Boring writes, "The number 144,000 is intended as symbolic theology, not literal mathematics. From our perspective it may sound limiting . . . and rather small; but in the ears of John's hearer-readers the number is stunningly large. Along with 'myriad' (literally 10,000), 'thousand' is the largest numerical unit found in the Bible. In biblical usage both are used primarily to mean 'a very large number' rather than to be taken with literal precision. . . . A multitude of 144,000 is meant to convey the impression of a vast throng

---

13. Harry O. Maier, "Coming Out of Babylon: A First-World Reading of Revelation among Immigrants," in *From Every People and Nation: The Book of Revelation in Intercultural Perspective*, ed. David Rhoads (Minneapolis: Fortress, 2005), 69.

14. See Clarice J. Martin, "Polishing the Unclouded Mirror: A Womanist Reading of Revelation 18:3," in Rhoads, *From Every People and Nation*, 91–92.

15. Jean-Pierre Ruiz, "The Revelation to John," in *The New Oxford Annotated Bible: New Revised Standard Version with the Apocrypha*, 4th ed., ed. Michael D. Coogan (New York: Oxford University Press, 2010), 2163.

beyond all reckoning (precisely the same as 7:9!)."[16] John is therefore referring to a vast multitude that is not quantifiable by human comprehension.

In attempting to identify the 144,000, Boring also argues that for John this symbolic number represents a continuation of Israel in the church: "The church in this picture is not only big, it is complete. The number 144,000 is a complete, fulfilled number. (The 144 is obviously the multiple of 12 x 12, the twelve tribes of old Israel and the twelve apostles of the new Israel)."[17] John's imagery of the church was therefore "complete" in that it represented a large and inclusive entity that was filled with both cognitive and identity diversity.

After establishing this diverse foundation in the first eight verses of Revelation 7, John writes, "After this I looked, and there was a great multitude that no one could count, from every nation, from all tribes and peoples and languages, standing before the throne and before the Lamb, robed in white, with palm branches in their hands" (7:9). In what is the assurance of ultimate salvation, invoking images of white robes and palm branches to symbolize righteousness and victory, John shifts the narrative from earth to heaven, where the richly diverse church triumphant worships God. Indeed, "As 7:1–8 presents the church militant on earth, sealed and drawn up in battle formation before the coming struggle, 7:9–17 presents the church after the battle, triumphant in heaven."[18] Revelation therefore shows that God intends the church—militant and triumphant—to be a place of diversity, inclusion, and welcome to the proverbial "Other."

John's message of liberation in Christ offers hope to many who are marginalized within and ostracized from modern communities due to race, ethnicity, gender, and social status. They too can find refuge in the diversity of the church. Indeed, as the discussion of Acts 2 in chapter 1 reminds us, the church was founded on the day of Pentecost, when Peter preached to a geographically, ethnically, and socially diverse group of Jews, a group rich in both cognitive and identity diversity.

16. M. Eugene Boring, *Revelation* (Louisville: Westminster John Knox, 1989), 130.
17. Boring, *Revelation*, 129–30.
18. Boring, *Revelation*, 131.

How Can Diversity and Inclusion Be Good in Moving the Church toward Reconciliation?

In addition to my conviction that God intends the church to be a place of diversity and inclusion, as evidenced in Revelation 7, I operate from the fundamental premise that the church—much like but more so than institutions of higher education—plays a special role in preparing people to address society's most vexing problems (recall the US Supreme Court's logic in *Fisher v. University of Texas at Austin* [2013], discussed in chap. 4). Indeed, in *The End of White Christian America*, Robert Jones argues, "In theory, a central part of the Christian Church's mission is to challenge its members to think beyond worldly perspectives and divisions. Churches are supposed to be sacred places where social distinctions that structure politics in the workplace melt away. This ideal permeates the New Testament scriptures."[19] Moreover, inasmuch as differences—including those of ethnicity, acculturation, gender, and sexual orientation—arise from different experiences, embracing difference also creates enormous opportunities for better understanding complex social needs (i.e., for understanding them better than homogeneous groups ever could).[20]

Moving the Church toward Reconciliation Requires That Social Divisions Be Addressed

While churches are typically associated with addressing social problems through missionary work and evangelism, they should also address some of the social divisions that have made society so polarized—including racism, sexism, and classism. Such bold approaches are necessary to move the church toward reconciliation.

On this point, Perkins implicitly calls for the church to return to her apostolic origins of diversity by highlighting an ongoing tension in the church: many argue that ethnic and social unity within the body of Christ (the *ekklēsia*) is a separate issue from the gospel. This is not scripturally sound. Referencing the Acts 10 narrative (discussed

19. Robert P. Jones, *The End of White Christian America* (New York: Simon & Schuster, 2016), 163.

20. Ross, *ReInventing Diversity*, 106.

in chap. 1) and describing what happens when God's vision for the church collides with culture, Perkins writes, "Man is sinful and does not easily give up his prejudices and dislikes. But again and again the Holy Spirit had His way and wrestled the people of God to submission on the issue of reconciliation."[21] What Perkins implies, my advocacy makes explicit: the church must return to her apostolic origins of diversity and inclusion by engaging in practices of reconciliation. In doing so, she will be an exemplar for society at large.

Perkins also calls on the church to have another Great Awakening to address her current issues of division, including those concerning race, and move toward reconciliation. After reminding readers of Peter's Spirit-inspired ability to move past racial and ethnic divisions and welcome Cornelius into the church, Perkins argues for the same type of Spirit-inspired reconciliation today. In describing each of the previous Great Awakenings in American history, he writes that "God used each of them to inspire movements aimed at healing the ills of society. . . . I'm praying for another Great Awakening where God shakes the Church in America and helps us to see the truth about race and how our misunderstandings have stained the vision."[22]

As discussed in chapter 4, racial divisions were the fuel for Nixon's southern strategy (a backlash to the Civil Rights Movement's progress toward diversity and inclusion). Racial divisions were also the genesis of the Republican Party's courtship with white evangelicals. Although race is only one issue, as the MAGA narrative and the deep divisions of 2020 revealed for the world to see, it remains a big issue in the United States.

Indeed, playing off Martin Luther King Jr.'s famous observation that eleven o'clock on Sunday mornings is the most segregated hour in America, Jones discusses the historical problem of racial divisions in churches while also arguing that racial reconciliation is built into Scripture and liturgy: "It's written into the lyrics of popular hymns like 'In Christ There Is No East or West.' The words of the hymn extol a vision of racial harmony—'Join hands, disciples of the faith, whatever your race may be. / All children of the living God are surely kin

21. Perkins, *One Blood*, 32–33.
22. Perkins, *One Blood*, 53–54.

to me.'—and its tune was the first African American music to be used in a white mainline North American hymnal."[23] He also laments that "however deeply the principles of racial equality may be enshrined in theology and liturgy, they have had little impact on the actual racial composition of Christian congregations, past or present."[24] Indeed, although Duke University's National Congregations Study found that the number of multiethnic churches has increased in recent years, increases in multiethnic congregations are far from parity in racial reconciliation.[25] Christians must be willing to address social issues, such as race, to move the church toward reconciliation.

Moving the Church toward Reconciliation Requires Cognitive and Identity Diversity to Address Issues and Solve Social Problems

Well-documented arguments support the conclusion that diverse groups are better at problem solving than homogeneous ones. In *Smart Mobs*, for example, Howard Rheingold describes how collections of people from diverse backgrounds are better at carrying out tasks and solving problems.[26] Similarly, in *The Wisdom of Crowds*, Jim Surowiecki shows that crowds of people can make accurate predictions.[27] Most salient, however, as Page considers the tasks of problem solving and prediction in *The Difference*, he specifically argues, "Diverse perspectives increase the number of solutions that a collection of people can find by creating different connections among the possible solutions."[28] If Page's premise is correct, then the church would most certainly benefit from a Revelation 7:9 kind of diversity and inclusivity in trying to solve social problems.

From an ecclesial perspective, the ability to do mission work and evangelism can only be improved by diversity. In *ReInventing Diversity*, for example, Ross tells the story of working in a strategy meeting with one of his client's otherwise homogeneous leadership

23. Jones, *End of White Christian America*, 163.
24. Jones, *End of White Christian America*, 163–64.
25. Jones, *End of White Christian America*, 165.
26. Howard Rheingold, *Smart Mobs* (Cambridge, MA: Perseus, 2002).
27. James Surowiecki, *The Wisdom of Crowds* (New York: Doubleday, 2004).
28. Page, *Difference*, 9.

teams. They had been working for hours to try to find a solution to a problem. At lunchtime, however, when an administrative team member brought in lunch, the chief executive officer noticed him staring at the board and asked, "Any questions?" The administrative team member said, "Yes, Why is this here instead of there?" The leadership team completely stopped because the administrator, who was not an insider or a part of the homogeneous group, had quickly uncovered a possibility no one else saw. In other words, the administrative team member's cognitively diverse vantage point allowed him to immediately see the impediment the group had been facing.[29]

The ability to better address social problems and provide sustainable, long-term solutions improves when the problem solvers share both cognitive and identity diversity. "People with different life experiences and training, people from different cultural backgrounds, likely see the world differently. And those differences—differences in perspectives—can be valuable when solving problems or making predictions."[30] I argue that this type of diversity is not only good for society; it is also what God intended for the *ekklēsia*.

In returning to Page's description of the differences between and importance of both cognitive diversity and identity diversity, consider the Gospels' descriptions of the disciples' respective backgrounds (cognitive) and the ethnic differences of the various Jews who formed the church on the day of Pentecost (identity). From a cognitive diversity perspective, although the pre-ministry occupations of the twelve disciples are not definitively known, we do know the disciples came from varying backgrounds. Peter, Andrew, James, and John were fisherman (Matt. 4:18, 21). Although fishing was a respectable vocation in Jewish culture, not all the disciples came from such noncontroversial occupations. Matthew was a tax collector (Matt. 9:9), a position that connected him to the Roman government as an agent of Jewish oppression. Simon the Canaanite (Matt. 10:4) was known as "the Zealot" (Luke 6:15; Acts 1:13), a title suggesting he may have been involved in political activities against the Roman government as a member of the Zealots, the

29. Ross, *ReInventing Diversity*, 201.
30. Ross, *ReInventing Diversity*, 16.

Jewish nationalistic party.[31] The apostles were clearly cognitively diverse because of their respective backgrounds, occupations, and experiences.

From an identity diversity perspective, the Acts 2 narrative describes the diversity of ethnicities that came together on the day of Pentecost to compose the church: "And how is it that we hear, each of us, in our own native language? Parthians, Medes, Elamites, and residents of Mesopotamia, Judea and Cappadocia, Pontus and Asia, Phrygia and Pamphylia, Egypt and the parts of Libya . . . , both Jews and proselytes, Cretans and Arabs—in our own languages we hear them speaking about God's deeds of power" (vv. 8–11). The church's apostolic origins show that its creation was rooted in God's deliberate embrace of diversity and inclusion.

With regard to cognitive and identity diversity, Page states, "If individual diversity contributes to collective benefits, we should pursue pro-diversity policies. Companies, organizations, and universities that hire and admit diverse people should not expect instant results. But, in the long run, diversity should produce benefits. . . . All else being equal, we should expect someone different—be their differences in training, experiences, or identity—to be more likely to have the unique experience that leads to the breakthrough."[32] If diversity and inclusion are good for secular organizations seeking to address social issues and are obviously part of God's original intention for the *ekklēsia*, the church has many reasons for pursuing reconciliation with multiple groups that she has historically excluded.

Evangelicals and the Issues: Can the Divisions Unearthed by MAGA Move the Church toward Reconciliation?

As shown in chapter 4, significant divisions now exist among American evangelicals because of Trump's personal character flaws and his politics. In attempting to answer the question, Where do we go from here? we need to note how some of the evangelical lines of division simultaneously create opportunities for cohesion in the church.

31. See, e.g., *Encyclopedia Britannica*, s.v. "Saint Simon the Apostle," https://www.britannica.com/biography/Saint-Simon-the-Apostle.
32. Page, *Difference*, 369–70.

As far back as June 2016, the evangelical advisers of then-candidate Trump included credentialed conservatives such as Ralph Reed, architect of the Christian Right's 1990s evolution toward pluralism and professionalization; James Dobson of Focus on the Family; Jerry Falwell Jr., then president of Liberty University; and Richard Land, formerly of the Southern Baptist Convention's advocacy forum. Noticeably, however, some significant holdouts included Russell Moore and the prominent evangelical magazine *Christianity Today*.[33] As Andrew Lewis writes, "Andy Crouch, executive editor of *Christianity Today*, published an editorial denouncing Trump: '[Trump] has given no evidence of humility or dependence on others, let alone on God his Maker and Judge. He wantonly celebrates strongmen and takes every opportunity to humiliate and demean the vulnerable. He shows no curiosity or capacity to learn. He is, in short, the very embodiment of what the Bible calls a fool.'"[34] Unlike Reagan, who solidified evangelical support, Trump is responsible for undermining the evangelical coalition.

Evangelicals appear to be divided regarding (1) individual rights versus communal morality and (2) differing opinions on cultural issues. After highlighting these issues, I illustrate how the church is moving and can continue to move toward reconciliation by providing an example of significant progress in a place where progress was originally improbable.

Differences among Evangelicals

Although evangelicals were not *politically* divided in 2016 (they overwhelmingly supported Trump on the *Roe v. Wade* issue), Lewis argues that "the election exposed an evangelical division over the proper way forward in a changing culture. Should evangelicals return to majoritarian, morality-based politics of the prior generation or pursue a minority, rights-based position?"[35] In other words, will evangelicals remain separate and advocate for a moral "high ground" (e.g., antiabortion advocacy), or will they move toward more mainline

33. See Lewis, "Divided over Rights," 80–81.
34. Lewis, "Divided over Rights," 81.
35. Lewis, "Divided over Rights," 77.

Protestant traditions in accepting individual rights, such as same-sex marriage?

In addition to this division over individual rights versus communal morality, evangelicals are becoming divided over cultural issues. Younger evangelicals in particular disagree with Trump's policies on immigration, his opposition to gay marriage, and his denial of the science evidencing climate change and global warming.[36] Indeed, although younger evangelicals remain more conservative than their nonevangelical Protestant counterparts, research shows that their greatest break with older evangelicals seems to be over their support for matters such as the environment and social welfare policies.[37] After surveying literature from a longer period of time, Jeremiah Castle writes, "Over the past three presidential election cycles, a number of popular and journalistic accounts have suggested that young evangelicals are becoming more liberal on a variety of issues and may be moving away from the GOP."[38]

What effect will the horrific killings of Ahmaud Arbery, Breonna Taylor, George Floyd, and the many others that have necessitated the Black Lives Matter movement have on evangelicals? What about the way Mexican Americans and Mexican nationals were racially profiled, shot, and killed at a Walmart in El Paso, Texas? What about the way migrant children were separated from their families at the US/Mexico border and locked in cages for indeterminate periods of time?

If the Nixon-created and Reagan-solidified relationship has become severable, evangelical divisions over such issues may present an opportunity for younger and more progressive evangelicals to build relationships with mainline Protestant groups and work together for social and civil reconciliation—for a more just, diverse, and inclusive society.

36. Elizabeth Dias and Jeremy W. Peters, "Evangelical Leaders Close Ranks with Trump After Scathing Editorial," *New York Times*, December 20, 2019, https://www.nytimes.com/2019/12/20/us/politics/christianity-today-trump-evangelicals.html.

37. Jeremiah Castle, "Subcultural Identity and the Evangelical Left: Comparing Liberal Young Evangelicals to Other Young Liberals," in *The Evangelical Crackup? The Future of the Evangelical-Republican Coalition*, ed. Paul A. Djupe and Ryan L. Claassen (Philadelphia: Temple University Press, 2018), 133.

38. Castle, "Subcultural Identity and the Evangelical Left," 124.

Moving the Church toward Reconciliation: Removing the Tension and Returning to Loving Relationships

While the church is divided over many issues, there is cause for optimism. Reconciliation is occurring in places where it would not have previously seemed possible. One example is Middle Church in New York City, a church that has been successful in creating a Revelation 7–type place of welcome for all. Middle Church, a predominantly white, conservative church that has grown by embracing diversity and inclusion, offers an example for how Christians might move forward in fulfilling the ministry of reconciliation that Jesus left to the church.

Middle Church is currently led by its first African American and first female pastor, Rev. Dr. Jacqui Lewis. The church's website indicates that the congregation places a premium on diversity in creating a place of welcome for all. Its "Who We Are" section states,

> The diversity of our congregation and staff looks like a New York City subway but it feels like a home full of love. Middle Church is where therapy meets Broadway; where art and dance meet a gospel revival; where old time religion gets a new twist. We are Bach, Beatles, and Beethoven; we are jazz, hip-hop, and spirituals. We are inspired by Howard Thurman, Ruby Sales, Fannie Lou Hamer, and Martin Luther King. We are on-your-feet worship and take-it-to-the-streets activism. We feed the hungry and work for a living wage; we fight for LGBTQ equality and march for racial/ethnic justice. We stand up for the stranger and the immigrant; we care for women's lives and Mother Earth.[39]

This congregation is committed to both cognitive and identity diversity. Yet as progressive and inclusive as Middle Church currently is, the church's history suggests it was probably the least likely place for reconciliation to occur.

The church was established after the Dutch West India Company sent Rev. Jonas Michaelius to the New Amsterdam settlement, on the southern tip of the island of Manhattan.[40] From very humble

---

39. "Who We Are," Middle Church, https://www.middlechurch.org/about.
40. Jones, *End of White Christian America*, 180.

beginnings, Middle Church grew to become the oldest continuous Protestant congregation in the United States, and it is currently co-affiliated with the United Church of Christ and the Reformed Church in America.[41]

Because of the church's location, over time the neighborhood changed, although the congregation did not. The neighborhood's German and northern European immigrants were replaced by Hispanics, Asians, young professionals, and artists. After chronicling the neighborhood's changes, Jones writes, "By the 1980s, Middle Church was in such bad shape that the Collegiate Corporation considered shuttering it altogether. Membership had dwindled to two dozen older white congregants, many of whom commuted into the city for services. It no longer had a community presence."[42] Circumstances necessitated that the congregation move in another direction. That direction ended up being a prophetic move toward reconciliation.

Under the leadership of Rev. Gordon R. Dragt, Middle Church deliberately "moved back into its neighborhood." It provided neighborhood artists with gallery and performance space, hired a jazz ensemble to play on the front steps of the church half an hour before worship services, and began community outreach targeted at local needs, including providing meals for people living with HIV/AIDS and affordable after-school childcare. "As new kinds of people began to attend church on Sunday morning, Dragt began to adapt the traditional liturgy to their interests. He removed the front row of pews to have more room for performers, and the church started a gospel choir, which turned out to be a vital entry point for many new members." As the church changed and moved toward reconciliation by finding commonality in Christ with diverse groups, its average Sunday attendance grew to exceed two hundred, with as many as four hundred in attendance on holidays.[43]

The congregation's success, resulting from its deliberate work toward reconciliation as it actively embraced diversity and inclusion, drew the attention of its current pastor, then a PhD candidate at

41. "Who We Are," Middle Church, https://www.middlechurch.org/about.
42. Jones, *End of White Christian America*, 181.
43. Jones, *End of White Christian America*, 181.

Drew University, who was called by the congregation in 2005.[44] Under Lewis's leadership, the congregation has developed an even stronger voice in addressing racial and social justice.[45] "Reverend Lewis provides a striking embodiment of Middle Church's transformation from a homogeneous white, elite congregation to an ethnically diverse community comprised of members who are gay and straight, well-off and down-on-their-luck, straight-laced and tattooed."[46] This is arguably the diversity that John wrote about in Revelation 7.

As someone who has done the deliberate work of reconciliation, I celebrate Middle Church's success and personally recognize how difficult it must have been. In working through Mission Reconcile's "Pathways toward Reconciliation" while previously leading Historic St. James AME Church, a majority Black congregation in downtown New Orleans, I partnered with Rev. Andrew Greenhaw, a dear friend and white pastor who previously led St. Paul's United Church of Christ, a majority white congregation in uptown New Orleans.[47] Although I am personally aware that Historic St. James benefited from whites and Hispanics who chose to join her in moving toward reconciliation during my tenure as the congregation's pastor, I can also appreciate that radical hospitality for "the Other" is not always extended by majority white congregations the way it was by St. Paul's in New Orleans.

Middle Church's pre-reconciliation history exemplifies King's axiom that eleven o'clock on Sunday mornings is the most segregated hour in America. In *The End of White Christian America*, Jones addresses this historical phenomenon, writing that "the work of desegregating churches will require some trailblazing both by majority-white congregations and by individual white Christians. At the congregational level, majority-white churches will need to initiate more cultural cross-pollination efforts, such as conducting joint services or initiating regular pulpit exchanges."[48]

44. https://www.middlechurch.org/our-leadership.

45. Jones, *End of White Christian America*, 183.

46. Jones, *End of White Christian America*, 184.

47. Anna Beahm, "Mission Reconcile Helps Southern Churches Dismantle Racism through Food, Fellowship," *Reckon*, April 29, 2021, https://reckonsouth.com/mission-reconcile-helps-southern-churches-dismantle-racism-through-food-fellowship/?utm_campaign=reckonalabama_sf&utm_source=twitter&utm_medium=social.

48. Jones, *End of White Christian America*, 193–94.

I can personally attest to the fact that such a recipe for success moves the church toward reconciliation and allows her not only to live out God's intention for the church but also to be an exemplar for society at large.

Conclusion

In this chapter, I answered the question "Where do we go from here?" by arguing that the church must go back to the principles of diversity and inclusion that were part of her apostolic origins if she is to move toward reconciliation.

The church has never been monolithic. Consequently, my advocacy is not intended to overly simplify the process of uniting factions within the body of Christ. The fact is, however, that for more than forty years, evangelicals have been far removed from mainline Protestant Christianity. For the first time in a long time, due to the extremity and enmity of the MAGA political narrative, divisions within evangelical Christianity have appeared. With deliberate work, Christians can build cohesions and move the church toward reconciliation in matters not limited to race.

Evangelical perspectives are changing, as is the conversation on race in America and the urgency for racial reconciliation. The diverse demographics of the many 2020 Black Lives Matter protests show that support for racial reform in the United States is widely shared. Because of her unique place in speaking to both matters of salvation in the "kingdom to come" and social inequalities in the "kingdom at hand," the church should be a part of leading the conversation. In other words, there is now potential to focus more on the ministry of reconciliation that Jesus left to the church by addressing the social and racial divisions that have been deliberately stoked by partisan rancor.

John's Revelation illustrates that God intends for the church—militant and triumphant—to be diverse and inclusive. Based on a principle from the secular world, it should be rich in both cognitive and identity diversity. If the church can return to an embrace of diversity and inclusion, as evidenced in her apostolic origins, she can be an exemplar for society at large.

The work of reconciliation is not easy. It remains a destination on the horizon. However, by putting theory into practice, it is indeed possible to move the church toward reconciliation. Scripture teaches that God is no respecter of persons. And that should empower us Christians in America to proclaim with consistency, and to show with our actions, that "we hold these truths to be self-evident, that all [people] are created equal."

EPILOGUE

> If you offer your food to the hungry
>   and satisfy the needs of the afflicted,
> then your lights shall rise in the darkness
>   and your gloom be like the noonday.
> The LORD will guide you continually
>   and satisfy your needs. . . .
> Your ancient ruins shall be rebuilt;
>   you shall raise up the foundations of many generations;
>   you shall be called the repairer of the breach. —Isaiah 58:10–12

Reckoning. Retribution. Repair. The year 2020 was unquestionably a year of reckoning in the United States, as the country was called to account for her past. If reconciliation is about bringing people together, 2020 was just the opposite. The year's events underscored several of America's most glaring divisions.

As evidence of America's continued racial divisions, the country saw a significant resurgence of the Black Lives Matter movement that underscored not only issues between law enforcement and minority communities but also the unconscious bias that so often surfaces to the detriment, and even mortal peril, of Black Americans. Further, as Ezra Klein highlights in *Why We're Polarized*, the very cemented divisions in America usually correlate with our identity politics and partisanship.[1] Even with an undeniable element of subjectivity in how white Republicans and Black Democrats view race relations in the

---

1. Ezra Klein, *Why We're Polarized* (New York: Avid Reader, 2020).

United States, surely a major public health crisis should have been common ground that could bring the disparate groups together. But it wasn't. In 2020, the COVID-19 pandemic drove Americans even further apart.

In the spring, after a novel variant of the coronavirus that scientists called SARS-CoV-2 hit the United States as part of a worldwide pandemic, President Donald Trump not only stoked racial divisions by repeatedly calling it the "China virus," but he also stoked partisan divisions by politicizing the issue of wearing masks. As epidemiologists' reports clearly showed that minorities were adversely affected more often than others, once again exposing ethnic disparities in economic resources and health care, Trump claimed that the virus would "go away, like magic," until he too contracted it, amid a series of super-spreader political events at the White House (large gatherings at which very few attendees wore masks).

As the handling of COVID-19 became voters' dominant concern in the lead-up to the November 2020 presidential election, Trump's repeated mishandling of the virus crisis and the hundreds of thousands of American deaths from the disease led to his plummeting popularity and eventual political demise. He would not go down, however, without a fight (and I mean that literally).

In the months leading up to the election, Trump and his political operatives made baseless allegations that the election results would be rigged against them. Sensing how many and how deep the political divisions were, and recognizing that Black Americans needed to be heard and represented, Joe Biden (the vice president under Barack Obama and the Democratic Party's nominee for president) made the unprecedented move of selecting a Black woman, US Sen. Kamala Harris, as his vice presidential running mate. The Biden-Harris ticket prevailed in an election that wasn't even close. In fact, Biden picked up the swing states Hillary Clinton had lost four years earlier. He even won the state of Georgia, a state Democrats had not carried since 1992.

The Biden-Harris coattails also helped elect Reverend Dr. Raphael Warnock—senior pastor of Martin Luther King Jr.'s home church, Ebenezer Baptist—as Georgia's first Black US senator. Moreover, Georgia also elected its first Jewish US senator, Jon Ossoff. These two were elected (it bears repeating) in the state of *Georgia*—a state that has long been known, unfortunately, as the home of a distinctly visible and persistent white supremacy. Even where division has long ruled, reconciliation is gaining ground.

While 2020 was, in general, a year of reckoning, the deadly fight Trump led on January 6, 2021, was about retribution. As the US Congress convened to certify the Electoral College's election results—with Trump's vice president, Mike Pence, as the presiding officer—Trump was simultaneously firing up a mob of his white nationalist supporters. Despite the fact that even Republican officials who publicly supported Trump were saying there were no major election irregularities, in the most unprecedented of moves, the then-sitting president of the United States spouted the angry rhetoric of "taking America back from her traitors" and encouraged the mob to act to protect America. A deadly insurrection followed.

After insurgents stormed the Capitol, waiving Confederate flags with "Trump 2020" and "Make America Great Again" insignia, they took over the office of Democratic House Speaker Nancy Pelosi as members of Congress either hid or fled for their lives. Indeed, several of the insurrectionists were heard screaming, "Where's Pence?" And there were reports that some of them intended to hang the vice president for refusing to acquiesce to Trump's repeated demand that he block the election certification. After a day of chaos, order was restored, many arrests were made, and on January 13, the House of Representatives impeached Trump for a second time. Although he was subsequently acquitted in the US Senate in the first-ever trial to convict a former president, those voting for conviction nevertheless contributed to what turned out to be the most bipartisan vote of its kind in the history of the republic. After the horrific day of retribution that was January 6 and the political fallout that stemmed from it, it seemed that things could not get any worse in our very *divided* states of America. The country was broken, and she was badly in need of repair. And a new administration was set to begin.

On January 21, 2021, the day after Joe Biden and Kamala Harris were inaugurated as president and vice president, Reverend Dr. William J. Barber II delivered the inaugural sermon at a special virtual prayer service livestreamed because of the COVID-19 pandemic. In preaching from Isaiah 58, he challenged Americans to move past their political and socioeconomic divisions to focus on justice and become "repairers of the breach." To again refer to King and chapter 5's salient question, Barber's thought-provoking and inspirational words really asked America, Where do we go from here?

Where do we go after this moment of racial reckoning that has unearthed so many and so deep divisions? Where do we go after an unpreceded insurrection and attempt to take over the government of the United States, at a time when domestic divisions seem to rival those that precipitated the Civil War? Where do we go after factions of the church seemed to succumb to her demons instead of being led by her better angels? These questions and many more will be answered by the way the church and society at large respond to Rev. Barber's challenge.

My prayer is that, in the years to come, we will look at America and see that we are all called to reconciliation, with the church leading the way as a model for justice, diversity, and inclusion.

AFTERWORD

If you're like me, then you might find yourself at this point taking a deep breath after reading all that Jay Augustine has shared here—and then realizing that you need to go back to page 1 and take it all in once more. Even as I made my way through his careful review of both the pernicious challenge of racism that we face and the scripturally grounded solution to it, I knew that his well-argued case for reconciliation calls for more than just a cursory reading and nodding of the head. What he says here needs to be truly absorbed and then acted upon.

Augustine acknowledges, "The work of reconciliation is not easy. It remains a destination on the horizon," but he shows why we in the church need to take on this crucial task by returning to our apostolic origins of diversity and inclusion. By guiding us through Scripture, first with Peter in Acts and then with Paul in Galatians, 1 Corinthians, and Romans, the author helps ground the practical principles of reconciliation in gospel faith. As the old hymn says, "There is a balm in Gilead," and it is this soul-medicine that truly can make a difference in this world in which we live. Augustine recognizes this, and he does a deep dive into the biblical texts before leading us on a journey through more recent historical events.

Indeed, it is the combination of scriptural investigation of social reconciliation and an honest historical appraisal of civil reconciliation in this country along with the subsequent reaction against it that makes Augustine's book particularly relevant for all of us who claim to be followers of Jesus of Nazareth and his way of love. He has shown us how effective the church's influence, primarily that of Dr. King and the Black church, was in the work that led to the Voting Rights Act of 1965. But he also has shown us the dark side of Christian influence, in a form of white evangelicalism coupled with the so-called southern strategy of the 1970s, giving rise in recent years to a virulent racism that has infected the soul of our nation while claiming to make it "great again." There are hard lessons for us in these pages. Augustine rightly says, "Owning America's truth is a requisite for moving toward reconciliation," but he also makes clear that we in the church must own our own truth and acknowledge our own complicity, however unintentional, in the divisions and violence that have erupted all around us.

Where this book ends, our work as members of the Jesus movement committed to reconciliation must begin. It is not enough to wag our fingers and shake our heads at politicians and media and secular leaders. Going back to our scriptural roots, we must indeed ask ourselves plainly what we the church should look like, what we can model to the rest of our country and our world. Dr. King once wrote, "Justice at its best is love correcting everything that stands against love."[1] Our way forward must be the way of love, which is indeed just and inclusive and unifying. Our agenda must be one that celebrates diversity, for as an old prayer puts it, God has created "all sorts and conditions" of people. Jay Augustine has done an excellent job in revealing how we got to this point and what is needed to move forward in a new way. Now it's time for us to take the necessary next steps.

The Most Rev. Michael B. Curry
Presiding Bishop and Primate of The Episcopal Church
author of *Love Is the Way* and *The Power of Love*

---

1. Martin Luther King Jr., *Where Do We Go from Here: Chaos or Community?* (1968; repr., Boston: Beacon, 2010), 38.

APPENDIX

Supreme Court Cases

Brown v. Board of Education (1954)
Fisher v. University of Texas at Austin (2013)
Gratz v. Bollinger (2003)
Grutter v. Bollinger (2003)
Northwest Austin Municipal Utility District No. One v. Holder (2009)
Plessy v. Ferguson (1896)
Regents of the University of California v. Bakke (1978)
Roe v. Wade (1973)
Shelby County v. Holder (2013)
South Carolina v. Katzenbach (1966)
Walker v. City of Birmingham (1967)
Yick Wo v. Hopkins (1886)

SCRIPTURE INDEX

SUBJECT INDEX